GW00862600

JOURNEYS OF THE
SWAN

JOURNEYS OF THE
SWAN

John Liley

CANALBOOKSHOP

JOURNEYS OF THE *SWAN*

John Liley

First published in 1971 by George Allen & Unwin (casebound)
and reissued in 1983 by Waterway Productions (perfect bound)

Second perfect bound edition 2015
published by
Canal Book Shop
Audlem Mill Limited The Wharf Audlem Cheshire CW3 0DX
www.canalbookshop.co.uk

ISBN 978-0-9574037-3-4

John Liley has asserted his rights under the Copyright, Designs and Patents Act 1988 to be identified as the copyright owner of the text in this book. The images and illustrations in this book are also subject to copyright; the various copyright owners are named in the Foreword.

Subject to very limited exceptions, the Act prohibits the making of copies of any copyright work or of a substantial part of such a work, including the making of hard or digital copies by photocopying, scanning or similar process. Written permission to make a copy or copies must be obtained from the publisher. It is advisable to consult the publisher if in any doubt as to the legality of any copying which is to be undertaken.

Foreword to this new edition

It seems like yesterday (or maybe the day before). The voyages described in this book took place in 1964 and '65 and were covered in articles by myself in *Motor Boat & Yachting*. Canals at the time had little public recognition, so to have them highlighted by an established magazine was something of a breakthrough. The articles attracted much correspondence and, for myself, the strident attention of officers of the British Waterways Board. That too represented an advance, for the policy until then had been aloofness.

British Waterways, far from being the protector of a system it held in the nation's trust, seemed bent on diminishing it. Local authorities disliked canals also. So the forces to be overcome were considerable.

Robert Aickman had been fighting the main battles; it was only through his work, tellingly recorded in the *Bulletin* of the Inland Waterways Association, that so much survives of our canal and river system today. In the wider campaigning that came later, and the blurring of history in holiday features and the TV programmes of recent times, Robert's contribution has been airbrushed out of the picture. But it was he, above all others, who saved our canals. My own participation was smaller, much smaller, but I trust I can suggest that the *Swan* and its saga helped in rallying the troops. Eventually the *Motor Boat & Yachting* pieces were incorporated in this book, which first appeared in 1971. By then the lobby for the waterways was really beginning to grow.

As to the *Swan* herself, the conditions on board would not be tolerated now – at least not by myself. In the hold, where I, and sometimes others, would spend each night, there would be drips from above. Then, somewhere on the lower Grand Union, these turned into a downpour as the covering overhead gave up the struggle for good. Inevitably this happened in the early hours of a Sunday, when locating a replacement within the shopping hours of the time was a puzzlement in itself. As our voyages continued, beds had to be carefully placed to avoid the bilge water, which invaded through holes in the hull and a slackness in the prop shaft bearing. From the timber of which the bottom was constructed rose a strong suspicion of rot.

The *Swan* provided adventure, and I hope this is conveyed in the text. In preparing this new edition it has been hard to resist tinkering here: youthful enthusiasm reigned when the narrative was first prepared, rather than flowing prose, but in making changes the excitement could have been lost. The book remains as originally produced, save for this introduction.

Acknowledgements are due, for photos used, to Hugh McKnight (pages 25, 27, 52, 66, 91, 132 Right); Harry Arnold (75 Right); Alex McMullen (156 Left); my brother Peter (44, 172 Right) and to Albert Barber who kindly drew the map.

Mary Gibby in 1982 acquired the *Swan* and restored her to first-class working order. It was a dream we could never have fulfilled and I, with many others, am grateful for the preservation of a vessel that might otherwise have faded away. I also wish to thank Peter Silvester and his wife Chris, of the Canal Book Shop of Audlem, on whose initiative this volume is republished, and who have undertaken the considerable work in preparing it for print.

Lastly I must acknowledge, again, the generosity of my friend John Sheldon, who owned *Swan* in the 1960s. It was John who paid the bills, and so very kindly allowed me to share in this exploration of long ago. Or was it yesterday, as I am still inclined to think?

John Liley, mid-summer, 2015

Publisher's note on photographs

This book was originally published in 1971, when there was no such thing as digital/electronic files. This edition has therefore been reset completely for printing. Most of the original photos were available and have been scanned, but a few had minor imperfections such as creasing or damage to edges - after all, they are nearly 50 years old. A few images had to be scanned from the original book, and the results of this process are never entirely successful, owing to the different technologies used then and now (old dots and new pixels do not seem to cohabit well). We have made every attempt to provide good quality illustrations, but apologise if a few are not quite up to the original standard.

Contents

Swan *at Tyrley, Shropshire Union Canal. The dwarf steerer is in fact stooped for a better grip on the controls*

Chapter 1

The *Swan*

Canals provoke a diversity of reactions. To some they are idyllic; to others, principally town dwellers, they form some kind of linear national gash bucket. Travel editors usually regard them as tranquil and quaint, though they are nowadays considered good fun, a viewpoint that was rare indeed, even fifteen years ago.

Hornblower had to work his passage through an English canal, while Mr Toad had a nasty experience on one. My own adventures began in 1952, when my father mustered his tribe, of which I was the youngest, and hired a boat. We visited Hoo Mill, Handsacre and Whittington Brook, all in what is technically an industrial area, although we had no means of telling this. Within yards of collieries we met cows, men with scythes and, on rare occasions, other boats, several of them horse-drawn; one, laden with coal, was called *Rose of Sharon*.

In due course we were ensnared in the arachnoid and fascinating labyrinth of waterways which then surrounded Birmingham. We were almost mown down by two trains of loaded coal boats, competing for a narrow bridge. My father, who had a talent for casual conversation, learned from a man with a sack across his shoulders that our boat was once called the *Little Wonder*. It had carried coal and had been his (the man's) own. This information was substantially incorrect, a fact we gleaned from a succession of further boatmen and keepers. In turn they would bestow different names, almost always claiming that the boat had once been their own. Obliquely they would compliment us by telling us what a grand craft our's had always been, ever since the day she was built (for them). These conversations usually began with the all-purpose canal gambit of' 'Owdyerdo', which was rarely uttered as a question. In the idle moments between locks, I would roll 'Owdyerdos' at quizzical cattle, sometimes varying this with the equally standard departure line of 'You're welcome', which, on the canal, always followed any word of thanks.

Suddenly our voyage went seriously wrong. We found ourselves engulfed in weed, much of it nightmarishly decayed. Such water as remained stank unequivocally. Our engine refused to run in these depressing circumstances, while the boat itself would barely float. It was my first taste of an abandoned canal.

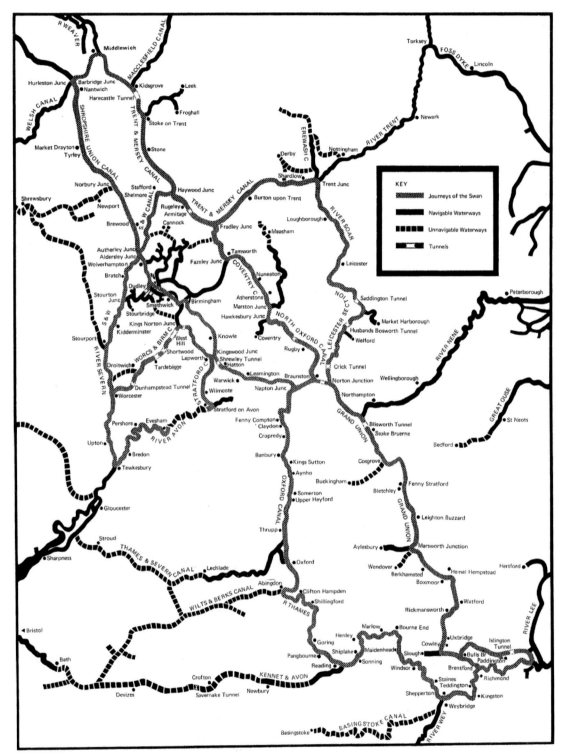

The Inland Waterways of central England

The abandonment had officially taken place a fortnight earlier. A celebrated broadcaster made the 'last' voyage. Following him, doubtless at a respectful distance, zealous workmen had started to drain off the water. This made life rather arduous for us. My mother and father were harnessed like drayhorses and made to march through stinging nettles. My brother, who was the strongest, vigorously poled and rocked the boat, while I myself, barely out of primary school, was appointed helmsman, by virtue of my lightness.

It never occurred to us to let the water back in again, for we were still unused to canals, particularly closed ones. There was just enough left to lubricate the muck and vegetation in which we chiefly ran. Fortunately, too, the locks still worked, albeit grudgingly. We found a wheelbarrow behind the gate of one and even discovered a lock keeper, to all intents and purposes as oblivious as ourselves to the official notice of closure. He joined us in a friendly gallop down the towpath when the rope broke at lock number four. By the end of the day, when we at last emerged into the heady waters of the Staffordshire and Worcestershire Canal, we had covered all of three and a half miles.

Early days. Stuck in the Hatherton Branch, Staffordshire, two weeks after closure, 1952. The weed lies thick; the water has largely drained away. Little remains of the canal today

In the late 1960s you could still see some vestigial remains of that waterway, the Hatherton Branch. A solitary lock stood in a field beside Watling Street, near Cannock. The rest had largely disappeared, desolated, like so much else in that region, by the gallumphing activities of the National Coal Board.

The Hatherton incident assumed heroic proportions in my mind and I have liked canals ever since. We took more holidays; later I bought a canoe in which, with an assortment of friends, I slugged about the waterways. Weedy canals we disliked, for our paddles tended to fling vegetation through the air, to land, not infrequently, upon ourselves. We preferred rivers and tried the Thames, a much more sanitary channel. Even here we had small troubles. At Chertsey our long suffering vessel was bitten by a horse, which beast continued to ransack our belongings throughout the night. Huge shadows would materialize on the tent walls; heavy breathing resonated in our ears. At five a.m. this fearsome animal rushed about the field, the, faint thundering noise gradually intensifying to a crescendo as a monster form crashed past the mouth of our frail shelter. As a final derisory gesture, the horse ate our bread, until then skilfully hoarded for the Bank Holiday. Beware of Chertsey.

Back on the canals, I found a boy of nine who could work fifty tons of cargo through a lock single-handed. I met a bull, also a boatman who shot other people's ducks. I voyaged through tunnels and the loneliest of cuttings. In addition, I felt the presence of ghosts, although I have never, to date, met one head on.

The series of voyages, which occupy the remainder of this book, began in 1964, when I met John Sheldon, an Admiralty scientist. He too had enjoyed some roistering forays in hired boats. He would show me pictures, often of girl friends, with some piece of canal antiquity vaguely discernible in the background. By this time I was on the editorial staff of *Motor Boat and Yachting*, a magazine devoted to boats, people, and occasionally to canals, although a colleague ominously informed me that 'anything about canals always leads to trouble'.

I had recently spent a year in ocean sailing, helping to deliver other people's yachts to or from the Mediterranean (a quite astonishing traffic exists). Equally often we had clawed our way around the British coastline in squalls or fog. I had learnt the true meaning of the words 'intense depression', 'bilge pump', 'that ship's going to pass pretty close', and the Morse Code for P ('your lights are burning badly'). Any trouble that canals might bring would make a welcome change.

John Sheldon had bought a boat. It was a 'narrow boat', the standard working craft of the Midland canals, and it was in rather a mess. It had carried coal, which was obvious. Before

Canal people at Aylesbury, Grand Union Canal

that, it had transported chemicals; these had done her no good at all, contriving to inflict a fair amount of corrosion. The boat had a name; it was *Swan*.

John found her in Michael Streat's yard at Braunston, a village near Rugby with roughly the same standing in the canal world as Brussels has to the Common Market. As John whittled his way down the price range, Michael Streat had said: 'Well, there is *one* other boat'. The other boat was *Swan*, still afloat by virtue of determined pumping, but unquestionably downtrodden. She had been brought there by some other enthusiasts, who had set upon her with gusto. One gay day, someone chipping scale in the hold chipped his way right through. A jet of water had entered, tools were hastily downed, and the boat forthwith abandoned.

John's student days were not too far behind him to be daunted by such minor matters as dirt and a wee bit of corrosion. We would 'do her up', zipping over her jaded surfaces with gleaming paint brushes. In a trice we would slap a cabin over her, and take her to Henley, for Regatta Week. There John·could luxuriate with his friends to the strains of stereophonic Wagner, pausing perhaps to take a hot bath, or, if the weather was kindly, to recline in a deck-chair on the cabin roof.

He bought the boat and two years later we went to Henley, still minus cabin. In truth there was too much other work to be done. Fresh plates were welded to the hull. The existing boatman's cabin, a leaky, bronchitis-inducing shadow of its former self, was 'made good', as the do-it-yourself books say, conjuring up visions of baptism or of black magic.

Swan had also at some time 'spread'. The majority of locks are 70 feet long by 7 feet wide. It is advisable, therefore, that a narrow boat should measure the same. The chains across the hold had at some time been allowed to fall slack; in consequence *Swan's* beam had expanded to 7 feet 2 inches. We were to learn this later.

Swan had been rubbing her way-around the waterways since 1934. She yielded various treasures of an appropriate vintage. Under the hatch in the bow was an old painted bucket of the type the boat people used to carry water. It had a hole in the bottom, and the name of another boat, *Rita*, painted on it. Despite an aura of the Dead Sea, the bucket still bore some discernible decoration, the traditional roses, and I now use it as a wastepaper bin.

In the cabin were more decorations, the equally traditional romantic castles, the origin of which no boatman can ever explain, although practically every narrow boat has them. Over everything was a patina of grime. The engine, which was accorded a compartment almost as large as the boatman's, reared menacingly through the dirt and rust. It stood chest high, a single cylinder unit festooned in tentacles and valves. Most noticeably, it had a large and archaic blowlamp, for pre-heating before starting.

John reckoned that we just had time to prepare the boat for the Festival of Boats and Arts at Stratford-on-Avon. It was a journey of forty miles and eighty-three locks, say two days' run, barring incident or disaster. We both knew, of course, how locks worked. We knew that their sluices were called 'paddles', which were frequently stiff and were best attacked aggressively with the 'windlass', a steel crank which could also serve as a jemmy or even as a weapon. We knew too the canal term 'gongoozler, an idle or inquisitive person who stands staring at anything out of the common'. This definition was printed in Bradshaw's Canals and Navigable Rivers, last published in 1928 and a holy grail for waterway devotees. Almost equally well-known in canal circles was 'chalico, a mixture of tar, cow hair and horse dung, made hot, used for filling up interstices in old wooden boats'. We employed this term in a quiz we cooked up in the *Motor Boat* office in order to enliven our readers' wintry soirées. Someone rang us up to complain that he couldn't find it in the Oxford English Dictionary, which, upon reflection, was an excellent reason to have used it.

John was determined, that we should not gongoozle, and, although he baulked at chalico, he decreed that we should paint the boat before we started, perhaps adding the projected saloon en route. Martin Johnson, another friend, would help us. Like an expeditionary force toiling into Khyber country, we set out from London in John's old Rolls Royce, trundling up the motorway laden with ladders, mops, pails, hardboard and paint.

Martin and I spent our first few days walloping scale in the hold. The sides were covered in it, and some rivets, if struck smartly, would yield fragments of shrapnel a quarter of an inch thick. We soon learned to work apart, on opposite sides of the boat. John confined his attentions to the cabin and its contents. He had managed only to cover the exterior with pink priming paint before he became distracted by more urgent matters, principally concerning the engine.

The first night aboard was hell, although the others thought it quite amusing. I had bought an inflatable mattress in London, selecting the right type with a deliberation which almost brought the shop assistant and myself to blows. Now, clutching this prize, I crammed myself, with the others, into the boatman's tiny cabin. This being only 12 feet long, and

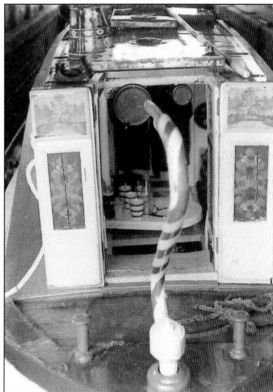

Above: *Dried out for repairs in the dock at Braunston*
Right: *The decorated doors and tiller. The big hand-wheel operates the gear change, the smaller wheel the throttle*

Blacking the hull at Braunston. Only the steel sides and stern are treated; the elm bottom is left unpainted and requires no protection, provided it is kept moist

already part occupied by a cast iron coal stove and a cupboard, had little room to spare for three people. Whole families used to, and still do, live in such a space, although most of the remaining working boats work in pairs, a motor boat towing an engineless butty; in addition, various enactments of Parliament control the number of people per cubic foot.

The first thing we did was to unfold a decorated cupboard door; this hinged down to form a bed that extended the full width of the boat. The second thing we did was to trap my inflatable mattress in the hinge and tear it, to the merriment of two-thirds of the crew. The manufacturers had thoughtfully provided a repair kit, but there their benevolence ended for they had omitted to include any rubber solution. In an atmosphere of panic, for it was midnight, I mistakenly applied insect repellent instead. Furiously, I goaded Martin out to his car, where excavation of the many strata of his tool kit failed to yield the necessary fluid. Finally he sealed the gap by trapping it between two pieces of wood, then clamped it tight with adjustable pliers. Martin has a great fondness for this device and will recount with pride how he once brought an Austin Seven back home with adjustable pliers clamped to the steering column, in lieu of the wheel, which had come off. Martin's student days are not far behind him either.

His repair was adequate, no more. Half way through the night the bed had gone down. In half the remaining time it had gone down again, and so on. The others awoke to find me permanently blowing like a demented tuba player; it was nearest I have ever come to sleeping on the hovercraft principle. I got up early, very cross and full of french chalk.

As a general boost to morale, it was decided to run the engine. This involved certain rites: a hunt for paraffin, a search for meths, and a close cross-examination as to why the matches were wet. The blowlamp itself had only two moods, dead stop and barely controllable eruption. John and Martin braved these furies while I watched from a discreet distance. From time to time Jack Monk, who then worked two of Michael Streat's cargo-carrying boats, would pass by and proffer sage advice. Old semi-diesels have a special esteem amongst the boat people, who in latter years have been compelled to grapple with more sophisticated but frequently temperamental units. The great merit of *Swan's* old Gardner, or of the legendary Bolinders, was that they were almost totally reliable. They shook, they coughed, and emitted a distinctive rattling note when running. Their basic attraction, of course, was that they did run, night and day, and would withstand brusque and frequently brutal treatment. A standard recipe for a dirty exhaust, for instance, was a fist-full of mothballs in the fuel tank.

Eight minutes' blowlamping was the minimum, so Jack assured us. The flame went out after seven and we proved him right. John started again, directing the flame onto the big

The boatman's cabin, John Sheldon facing the camera. The table also hinges upwards to act as a cupboard door

steel bulb on top of the cylinder. Then, taking a short bight of rope, he looped it round a retractable stud in the rim of the flywheel and pulled. On the rebound the engine fired. There was a rush to the controls, for the Gardner had to be started in forward gear and at full throttle; out of the corners of our eyes we could see the mooring ropes twanging and other craft bobbing like corks in the wash.

The engine noise was just as I remembered it from the narrow boats I heard in the early 1950s. There were many more boats then, and many more single cylinder diesels. That unique *ptock,ptock,ptock* sound brought waves of nostalgia. I am normally completely unaffected by engine noises; in fact I regard the internal combustion principle with some alarm. I nonetheless cherish memories of narrow boats echoing through the gaunt cuttings of central Birmingham or mowing along the wild windswept stretches of the Shropshire Union. *Swan's* engine note was just the same.

Gingerly we took her down to the junction, where the North Oxford and Grand Union canals meet. Here elegant cast iron bridges carry the towpath across the water. Beneath

The single-cylinder Gardner semi-diesel

is a triangular island, the apex of which once contrived to puncture, and effectively sink, a boat loaded with concrete piles. Spots such as this, where a 70 foot boat can turn round, are surprisingly rare on the canals. The turning process itself is known as 'winding', pronounced with a short 'I', as in windy.

We winded, and at this juncture discovered that reverse gear, which constitutes the brakes of a boat, was, in *Swan's* case, somewhat woolly. We returned to base even more cautiously than when we left, for we now fully realized our damage potential. Jack diagnosed a lack of ballast at the stern and politely inferred that if the propeller was deeper in the water it might stand a fighting chance.

Although the airbed had been restored to health, we still lived in a modicum of discomfort. I was obliged to return to London that evening, and, by doing so, would raise the living standards of the other two by roughly thirty-three per cent. Before leaving, I arranged to rejoin them at Stratford, where I had to cover the Festival for *Motor Boat and Yachting*.

I journeyed home from Rugby by train, covered in grime and iron oxide and trying as hard as I could to readjust to the modes and manners of my fellow travellers. Comfortable though my compartment was, it had an uneasy atmosphere, probably engendered by the reaction to my wild appearance. I walked down the corridor for a wash, and wished I could join the others at the start of *Swan's* new career on the canals.

Chapter 2

Expedition to Stratford

Of the several railway companies which busied themselves with waterways during the last century, the Great Western must surely take the wooden spoon, for its malice and its general ruffianism. One of the worst cases of all was that of the Upper Avon, which lay between Evesham and Stratford and which, until 1860, had been sound both in wind and in limb. At that juncture it was purchased by a Mr Boulton, who, too late, was discovered to be a railway nominee. Thirteen years later the waterway was derelict. Mr Boulton had disappeared in the interim and with him went any hope of redress.

There is a canal at Stratford too. This also benefited from Great Western benevolence, coming to what seemed a sticky and stinky end in the 1920s. Legally it remained navigable, even if practical obstacles, such as a dearth of lock gates and rampant arborescence, rendered any serious voyage impracticable. This tedious situation ended when, in 1964, the canal was reopened in melodramatic circumstances, of which more anon.

Thus *Swan's* maiden trip under new management was down to Stratford, to celebrate the reopening, in company with a mixed bag of 200-odd other vessels. Anthony Leonard had joined her crew, bringing with him a device which he referred to, in all seriousness, as 'the motor bicycle'. Why he stuck to such archaic terminology was beyond us, but he had for his machine a concern which knew no bounds. This was directly proportional to the inconvenience it caused the rest of us. The ensuing days seemed largely spent in hoisting the motor bicycle from the hold, under careful direction from Anthony, so that he could reconnoitre fish and chip shops or seek out public houses. These institutions located, the crew would trundle off on foot nursing areas of contact with the kick-starter or the handlebars.

I arrived in Stratford by train, shoed and be-suited, as befits a gentleman of the press. As I had a shrewd suspicion of what was going to happen, I had brought some old jeans as well. With me came Margit, a young lady from Germany, and a friend of both John and Martin, although she had yet to become acquainted with canals.

We found Stratford in turmoil, full of boats, policemen, traffic jams and tourists. *Swan* wasn't there, although, as we were told, shortages of water up the canal were delaying

Characteristic split bridge at the entrance to the Stratford Canal at Lapworth. The slot in the centre permitted towlines to pass through without being unhitched

sundry pilgrims. The army, which had been involved in the restoration, had laid a field telephone up the towpath; two youths were manning it. '*Swan*? No.' I described the boat: long, unconverted, cabin painted in undercoat. 'Oh, you mean Pink Primer. She's on her way down now. Margit and I set off up the path. Every few minutes we met a boat, its occupants often dirty and glowering defiantly. Soon we were out in the country, scrambling towards the locks down from Wilmcote. A faint popping noise drifted over the hedgerows and *Swan* appeared, manned by chimney sweeps. As I climbed aboard, I got a black oily streak down my coat. The engine, it seemed, did not accurately combust all its fuel.

Yes, there were water shortages, mainly caused by the glut of craft. Each boat moving down to Stratford took a lock full of water with it, making life that much harder for the next fellow. Some boats had stuck. One, indeed, had refused to let anyone past and some hot words had been exchanged. Hence, I gathered, the looks of militant zeal from those we had met on the way up.

Worst of all were the consequences of the boat's swollen girth. Two of the locks had been exactly the statutory 7 feet, a fact unnoticed until Martin let the water out, wedging the boat between the inward bulging walls. A lot more water had been wasted in employing

Above: *The Stratford Canal before restoration: locks on the Wilmcote flight*

Right: *During restoration, with one of the sidewalls cut back for relaying by prison labour*

the old canal trick of attempting to flush the boat from each lock. A lorry had damaged its clutch in pulling and the chains across the hold had fallen so slack that links could be removed from each of them. Despite these indignities, the crew had won through, although none of us dared think too hard about repeating these performances on the journey back.

The Queen Mother was to perform the reopening ceremony the next day and the lock from which she was to be ferried was closed for the painting and decorating which is customary on these formal occasions. We were therefore condemned to a night in Stratford in the least salubrious part of the entire canal. An officious youth conveyed this information in a terse harangue from the bank. Everyone swore and set about banging mooring stakes into the knobbly towpath alongside.

My suspicions about conditions aboard had been confirmed, compelling a change into jeans and jersey, which I wore for the remainder of the week. A tent had been erected in the hold for Margit, and I was to sleep under canvas in the bows, beside the lavatory. More friends had arrived, bringing with them a voracious baby; with great wisdom they had decided to sleep ashore, though whether they booked their hotel before or after seeing the rest of us I never did discover.

Somehow we could all pack ourselves into the boatman's cabin, in order to brew up over the primus. The original coal stove, still installed, had shown itself the means to an early grave, by dint of a ready output of dioxide. Emblazoned on its ironwork were the words 'The Hostess Range' . This brought fits of girlish glee from Margit; 'hostess' apparently meaning something slightly different in Germany.

I first went to Stratford as a member of a horrific coachload of schoolchildren, ostensibly eager to see Redgrave as The Merchant. We discovered the Avon first, for the portion past the Memorial Theatre has always remained navigable, and we launched ourselves upon it in chartered skiffs. The canal, however, was a goner; there seemed little doubt about that. It was a byword amongst those who cared (at that time very few people indeed). Although a lock stood smack in front of the theatre, it was unworkable. Stratford council had installed a footbridge across it and, in the basin just above, an ornamental fountain loomed spikily from the shallows.

A pre-Festival jam. Boats queue at Wilmcote

One of the first things that I ever discovered about canals was that they had to be fought for. Quite contrary to standard empire-building techniques and the trappings of power mania, those in control of the waterways seemed the most anxious to get rid of them. The Lower Stratford was only one of many which had been nationalized in 1948. From that date onwards many of the waterways were administered under the blue and yellow banner of British Waterways, the official representatives of public ownership. Notwithstanding, the system continued to deteriorate, often grotesquely, and in defiance of statute, public enquiry and the lessons of the Continent. The toll system and the standards of the turnpike remained, traffic was actively discouraged.

I knew whose side I was on. The whiff of battle had reached me, even as a child. As John Smith, M.P. for London and Westminster was later to say, 'These still waters are strongly laced with arsenic. To stir them up at all is to stir up the wildest of passions.' The passionate were led by Robert Aickman, who in 1944 had formed the Inland Waterways Association

Canal cottage on the Lower Stratford

David Hutchings (left) with Robert Aickman

and had campaigned with energy and a compelling oratory. The power of his writing was bewitching and I never knew him bested in argument, even when confronted with the biggest guns of officialdom. One day the seventy odd *Bulletins* of the IWA, written almost in their entirety by Robert Aickman, will be more widely recognized as the *tours de force* they were.

That we were all in our distinctive ways devouring chipped potatoes on *Swan's* cabin top and in the lee of a Stratford warehouse was due to the labours of David Hutchings. It was he who plunged, at times literally, into the task of shifting 300,000 tons of mud from the thirteen mile waterway and of restoring thirty six locks that, in law, should never have needed restoring.

Had Ealing studios continued to exist as a unit making feature films, they would have found much material in the restoration of the Lower Stratford Canal. It had all the necessary ingredients of heroism, comedy and drama. Closure, which was mooted in 1958, was thwarted by the discovery of a sixpenny canoe ticket, haplessly issued by a British Waterways clerk within the necessary preceding period of three years (the law has since been adjusted). John Smith wrote an estimated 20,000 letters in two years and persuaded the National Trust to take responsibility. The required £50,000 was raised within a few weeks. Estimates for abandonment had been twice that sum, although the excuse given for taking this course was a saving of £7,000 on a bridge at Wilmcote. Stratford Corporation resisted the whole venture, objecting on various grounds, including the wastage of public money and that 'the tranquility of the gardens will be disturbed by the noise of power-driven craft' (the A34 main road clamourously borders the same gardens).

Even in the centre of a town, a night in the hold of *Swan* can be an entrancing experience. It is undoubtedly more spartan than the cosy cabin of a cruiser, but it is far less claustrophobic and is the best of all planetariums. Distant galumphing noises from the cabin reminded me of the cramped mayhem I had managed to miss.

The following morning we moved toward the Memorial Theatre, hounded by a great fleet, and aided through the locks by prisoners from Winson Green, Birmingham. They, together with the servicemen, had done much of the heavy work in the restoration. It had proved a great idea to use them, a mutually beneficial technique that deserved extension. One of the prisoners mentioned his normal task when interned; sticking the metal ends on boot laces.

We chugged out into the Avon to find the banks lined with craft and all the best berths gone. John was directed way downstream to a point beside a notice which stated GREAT DANGER WEIRS. Someone had painted a large letter Q in front of the W, and we were also surrounded by venomous vegetation.

Stratford at night, from below the Avon weirs

Our fellow visitors were a varied lot. Possibly we were the most squalid, although we could claim that this had been forced upon us; had we stayed to smarten the boat up, we would never have made Stratford at all. Other crews varied from some elderly ladies, complete with buttered scones and china tea service, to further amateur narrow boaters, better versed in the traditions than ourselves. They wore peaked colliers' caps and, in several cases, earrings; some played the concertina.

Condemned, like ourselves to outer Never Never land, was another narrow boat, the *William*, which had come from Beauchamp Lodge Boys' Club, Paddington. She carried some very tough kids indeed. Their warden, a rotund, genial figure with a red beard, was Mr Jewiss, almost always referred to as Bosun, or Bose. Later I got to know Dennis Jewiss quite well and was to see what a tremendous job he did. Each year he took groups of children on trips in the *William* penetrating to the remotest and obscurest fastnesses of the canal system. He could face the most alarming events with great sang-froid. 'What's that boy doing up there?' he would say, gazing at a tiny face peering from amidst the gantries and pipes of a power station, 'Not one of ours is he?' He virtually lived for the club; in fact he and his family had a flat at the top of Beauchamp Lodge, where he presided benignly over its energetic membership.

Rallies of boats are a big feature of waterway campaigns. Their main function is to encourage the use of some neglected or threatened artery (it is always crisis year on the canals). Their locations are chosen with great precision and the main pleasure is in the going. The Stratford affair was actually termed a Festival of Boats and Arts and it was everything a rally should be. There were fireworks across the river, accompanied by Handel; there were exhibitions, a floating stage, ballet, and jazz (my own private fetish). There was also an impromptu non-musical performance by the orchestra, which looked like whirling downstream on its raft while the conductor tramped haplessly through the flower beds.

The Queen Mother charmingly performed the reopening. Hutchings got an M.B.E. and the prisoners planted some roses beside Lowsonford Lock to commemorate their own substantial part in the proceedings. Of the restoration Hutchings said 'Fortunately none of us were experts, or we should have known it was impossible.'

The proceedings were rounded off by the 1812 Overture, with twenty five pounder contributions from the Artillery. We sat on the fringe of a tree-lined bowl downstream of the theatre to watch the guns flash on the opposite bank.

Our journey back was not uneventful. We stuck in lock forty-four having entered full tilt in an endeavour to overcome the constriction in the walls. Simultaneously we acquired

The re-opening. Crowds line the basin near the Memorial Theatre

some wire around the propeller and I was dangled unceremoniously by the ankles in order to free it. A lorry, with a block and tackle, hoisted us in.

We spent a blissful evening in the countryside at Wilmcote and I left by train for London the next morning. The others had a rough passage, I heard, for they were held up by other boats as the water shortage intensified. This situation largely stemmed from the odd arrangement of locks at the Grand Union end. There was at one time a lot of back-biting between different canal companies and when the Stratford and the Grand Union were joined, it was insisted that a single lock be built in the connecting link. Every boat going down to Stratford took a lockful of water with it, let down another lockful on return and lost yet another if it elected to use the connection through to the Grand Union.

I wrote a laudatory account of the reopening for *Motor Boat and Yachting*, receiving for my pains two indignant letters from readers who felt I should have bitched about the whole thing, on the grounds of the hardships suffered en route. As it had been blazing hot and as no 30 foot waves had been about to sweep us from the map, I judged the hardship angle rather over-rated. Anyway, I felt in a reasonably good position to appreciate the hazards. Upon reflection, most of us had enjoyed them.

Left: *Cast iron aqueduct at Bearley, five miles up from Stratford*
Below: Swan *going home: John and Margit take it easy*

Chapter 3

Back Home

It took so long to extract the boat from the Stratford Cut that the captain's holiday had almost gone. There was an incautious endeavour to make up lost time and *Swan* had completely failed to negotiate a tight bend south of Braunston. The bows careered through some shrubbery to inflict a hearty blow upon the canal bank. Those aboard did a brisk run forward upon impact, voicing various complaints and condemnations as they went. By means of some vigorous poling, the boat had been wrested free, leaving a dent in the earth reminiscent of a meteorite crater. It was still visible a year later.

In Blisworth Tunnel, three thousand yards of unspeakable gloom and dampness, the headlight had gone out. The steerer, thus distracted, had contrived to scrape the boat along one wall. He scraped with it Anthony's motor bicycle, discarding number plates, lights and other bric-a-brac as he went. The machine was at that time being carried transversely on a primitive deck, the main intention being to avoid the ugly riot scenes on unloading. In this position it underwent a scarcely discernable but relentless erosion against the walls of tunnels and the sides of locks.

John left the boat at Leighton Buzzard, his time having run out. We had still to reach Cowley, a spot near Uxbridge where a permanent mooring had been negotiated. There, no doubt, the cabin could be briskly added, the Hostess torn out by its rusty roots and various other drastic modifications conducted.

A group of us went up to Leighton the following weekend and proudly brought the boat back in a single day, the hottest of the year as we sweatingly discovered. The route across the Chiltern Hills is peppered with locks, and provides a rare test for dissipated lungs and limbs. Because Grand Union locks are twice the width of a narrow boat, we were in no great danger of getting stuck. The experiences near Wilmcote had, in any event, presented an unparalleled opportunity of hardening in the chains. These were now twanging away like guitar strings and, thus corsetted, we were shrinking back to a proper size. Rarely in future were we to find ourselves wedged between lock walls and on the verge of tears.

We had started from Leighton at five a.m. and went 'til dusk, the engine's output of exhaust growing progressively more fulsome as we went on. Towards the end, lumps of soot the

Above: *Margit descends the Chilterns. In the background: the lock sill, something of a hazard as the water level drops.* Right: *Lock wheeling. The bike is only used on longer flights.*

size of sugar lumps were spraying into the air, often landing on people's heads, where they would glow briefly before expiring as oily blobs.

'Use your wheel, boy, if you've got one', a boatwoman called as we careered by the moored *Lucy* and *Ian*, two of Michael Streat's boats. The wheel referred to was the throttle control, or 'speed-wheel' as the boat people tended to term it. They have always been great moralisers on other people's bad behaviour, particularly on speeding past moored craft. Nonetheless, the boat people, as a race, are not beyond carving up whole platoons of cruisers themselves, leaving them waving in the wash like a kite tail, the air rent by crashing crockery and the cries of the coffee-stained.

We really had the bit between our teeth and, once it became apparent that we might reach Cowley that day, no-one was spared. Margit tried to take a swim at King's Langley and was almost left behind. We took turns to ride ahead on John's old cycle in order to prepare the locks. An at times nebulous towpath and some skilfully camouflaged anglers made these rides an adventure on their own. The brakes were bad too; on several occasions a gaggle of gongoozlers would be dispersed by the arrival of a whirling figure who, on attempting to dismount at 10 mph, would frequently sprint some way down the slope beyond the lock.

Our injuries mounted, for locks have many appurtenances, but we made steady progress. We later learned that Leighton to Cowley was an average day's run for a pair of loaded boats. The boatmen have many tricks and short cuts, some of them a bit rough on the

Jim Collins, Blue Line boatman, on the coal run to Southall

Rose decoration, painted by Ron Hough at Braunston Dock

Measham ware, made between 1870 and 1920 and in commom use by canal families. Seen in a window in Bond Street, London, 1966

equipment. They nonetheless manage to travel without the hysterical aura of our own progress.

Cycling ahead to prepare the locks is a rite of long standing. Usually conducted by the younger members of a crew, the practice is known as 'lock wheeling'. The term also embraces those who slog on by foot, urged on by the concomitant noise of the boat as it devours the locks just behind. In these conditions the word 'pound', denoting any stretch of·water between locks, takes on a meaningful ring. Ironically a long pound causes no trouble for here no-one bothers to wheel. It is a succession of short pounds which catalyse exhaustion and mutiny.

The waterway vocabulary is a distinct one. Thus the canal is almost always 'the cut'. Marsworth, the magnificent reservoirs of which we had passed in the early morning, is known, for some reason, as 'Maffers'. Port and starboard are never referred to, just 'left' and 'right', while 'back' and 'front' are also in common usage. There is a strict etiquette too. Because the canal life is of necessity somewhat public, it is an unwritten law never to stare into a cabin. The boat people must not be openly regarded as oddities, nor are they 'bargees'. They live on 'boats' (a barge is twice as wide).

John winding upper gate paddles, near Marsworth

The narrow boat fraternity, the professionals that is, had dwindled to a handful since the heyday of the canals in the early nineteenth century. The survivors were still living in the cramped conditions I have indicated, boatmen being forced to bring their families with them when railway competition became really intense, roughly a hundred years ago.

The rose and castle decorations evolved shortly after, probably as a means of offsetting mundane cargoes. Other traditions were also established, such as the magpie penchant for brass, including the three rings round the stove chimney, polished to within an inch of their lives.

Canal people work hard, exceptionally hard by the standards of today. There are few lock-keepers to lend a helping hand and the sight of a mother of six whirling the chronically stiff paddles at Hatton or Knowle is reminiscent both of ancient Britain and modern Russia.

Loaded pair coming south up the Braunston flight, 1965

Despite their many hardships, they were still, at that time, an attractively close-knit, if insular, group. I was not surprised to read a few years ago that the children of the canal families then remaining, although schooled in a Birmingham hostel stuffed with modern comforts, preferred, almost to a child, the life on the boats. School was much to claustrophobic.

Horse-drawn narrow boats during a stoppage for repairs on the Grand Union in the 1930s

We met a pair of the Willow Wren Company's boats, blasting out of Rickmansworth lock in an inferno of sound. A great column of blue-black smoke shot high in the air, as the motor boat moved forward and smote the uppermost gates apart. They slid past us, fully loaded with food extract in barrels. The towline snaked out and the motor cracked into life again as it took the strain. We rated a smile for our soot-spotted demeanour, as the boatman's wife leaned out on the heavy tiller of the butty.

More friends had come to welcome us at Cowley. A triumphal party hoisted the motor bicycle onto the towpath and someone fell into the hedge. We then repaired to The Shovel, an admirable little pub near the lock. Here in a mirror we saw ourselves as others had been seeing us; we looked abominable and John resolved to give the engine exhaust the topmost priority in the projected winter refit. We also decided that the hats we had so much derided at Stratford-on-Avon, were, in fact, a necessity. Not only was our hair besmutted and slightly charred, it was also quite inadequate as protection against the blows of fortune. Beneath the cabin roof were the control rods, running forward to the engine. These consisted of the speedwheel and another larger wheel, for operating the gear change, plus a nasty little handle for trimming the fuel injector. This was always in the 'on load' position, i.e. pointing down, whenever I happened to stand up. As a result my head was becoming a mass of scar tissue. I now knew why hats were almost *de rigeur* for boatmen; those who didn't wear them seemed possessed of a boxer's reflex, ducking the slightest hint of assault.

The motor bicycle was temporarily abandoned, pending various repairs and the attachment of new lights. Anthony thus joined us in a nervy journey back to Hammersmith by van. The canal metabolism had accustomed us to a different pace, with greater inevitability of momentum. We were quite unused to brakes and found the Chiswick roundabouts quite shattering. It made canal travel all the dearer to us; we resolved to make another journey before the winter set in. This would be a circumnavigation of London: down the Regents Canal to the docks, then back up the Thames, to rejoin the Grand Union at Brentford.

Chapter 4

London

The exploration of London by canal may be likened to a journey along that partial misnomer, the Underground Railway. There is, of course, a welcome absence of ticket collectors, although the passengers are not immune from rain, soot, or the flakes of bricks from bridges. It is advisable, too, to take some sandwiches, for a complete circuit by water takes roughly two days.

You board your vehicle in an outer suburb, say Uxbridge, then slowly tootle inwards, just as the tube does. The number of passengers is at first few, but will in time increase, as your friends trot in from the side streets, braying for guidance from the natives. The points of interest, a trickle at first, gradually become more frequent as the centre approaches. Southall, Northolt, Alperton and Kensal are all several miles apart and there are no locks. But at Camden the tempo suddenly quickens; passengers will pour aboard at Hampstead Road Locks (nowhere near Hampstead Road, as far as I can make out). From then on you're in London proper with a bonus of two tunnels, at Maida Hill Tunnel, a mere 272 yards, and at Islington, over half a mile long.

We spent our first night to all intents and purposes in the Zoo. The Regents Canal passes right through it, in an impressive cutting. Men on passing lighters may exchange stares with flamingoes or, on rarer occasions, a perambulating elephant. It was in this unique Doctor Doolittle territory that *Swan* was moored.

Double locks on the Regents Canal, a great place for timber yards

To visit the Zoo is one thing, to hear it another. I had previously associated the surrounding houses with a certain exclusivity but now deduce an abundance of double glazing or of romantic jungle-loving personalities. It is at night that all the creatures we don't normally see decide to wake up. They include an intermittent circular saw-type animal, another which tears up calico and something else (a bird?) with a random and quite shattering output of horror film screeches.

The Zoo portion of the Regents Canal is perhaps the most exotic stretch of the London Circuit, although the penetration of the north west suburbs, which we had achieved the day before, is not without its moments. There is an aqueduct across the North Circular Road in NW10, an unexpected golf course at Sudbury and, nearer to the heart of things, the discovery of Little Venice, Paddington. Here is a substantial basin, part of which was municipalized some years ago to make a dreary little garden that nobody sits in. There are luxury flats, some gay houseboats in the adjoining stretches, and the junction with a short arm to Paddington. Beside this, in a bedlam of beat groups, stands Beauchamp Lodge, an old, long-suffering building, which accommodates the boys' club and is Dennis Jewiss' stronghold.

We had earlier asked a British Waterways official if we could moor *Swan* here for the previous week; apart from two waterbuses and an island, the basin was starkly under-occupied. The reply, in the negative, was backed up in startling terms, 'Good Lord no. If we allowed that everyone would want to come.' We were not allowed to mingle with the adjacent houseboats either, hence our eventual hectic schedule and the stop at the zoo.

We were to be joined in our circular tour by some twenty other boats, the *William* amongst them. It was all an IWA idea, an endeavour to keep the locks open at weekends, which at that time they rarely were, being padlocked outside normal working hours.

With many Paddingtonian 'Yarroos' and other war cries, the *William* bowled in from the west. I could dimly discern Dennis Jewiss beyond a sea of faces on the cabin roof. The *William* struck the lock gate squarely and smartly. Everyone on the roof fell over and Mr Jewiss who as helmsman could properly see for the first time, reintroduced himself.

All the way down to Limehouse the locks are duplicated and stand in pairs side by side. *Swan* and *William* bundled into one and the flock of cruisers into the other. Many hands spoilt the broth, so to speak, upon the lock machinery and in due time we edged towards dockland. Rising and falling like the tones of the sea, an endless hubbub emanated from the boat next to ours. The *William* could not have been more aptly named, for Richmal Crompton personalities abounded aboard, often tougher, even dirtier than their prototype but invariably characterful. This time there were several extra passengers, including a

Locking through at St. Pancras. Alongside the William. Dennis Jewiss, right, has his breakfast

Into the City. The buildings crowd closer, the shadows deepen. The engine echoes from the bridges and jaded warehouses

Islington Tunnel is 960 yards long and has no towpath. Lighters must be pulled through by tug

number of girls, diligently washing up, cooking, washing up and falling over as each obstacle to progress was encountered.

City Road Basin, factory-encumbered, yet deserted, was reached five locks down. The Jewiss brigade who had been here before, sneaked off to the left, where the main channel lies. Innocent and oblivious, I duly took *Swan* into the basin, for the correct route is not apparent from within the lock. Amidst much revving and admonishment we extracted ourselves and set off in pursuit of the *William*.

The basin was the site of the formal opening of the Regents Canal, which took place in 1820. Here a boat from Paddington, also named *William*, was the first to land its cargo, which included the inevitable beer, consumed upon the spot with equal inevitability.

The new waterway, extending eight miles from Paddington to Limehouse, had taken eight years to build. Commercially it was a failure and its construction had been attended by many difficulties, not the least of which were fisticuffs with the staff of William Agar when the workmen entered that person's estate at St Pancras. A gentleman named Congreve also created some difficulty by erecting a 'hydro-pneumatic double-balance lock' at Hampstead Road; it leaked, was slow and, after an expensive legal fracas, was eventually dismantled. John Nash, the architect, emerged from this ruck untarnished, as he deserved to do, being a most active promoter of the works.

The Regents Canal hit the headlines again in 1874 when the boat *Tilbury*, laden with explosives, blew up with devastating effect beneath Macclesfield Bridge. Three lives were lost, buildings were wrecked and animals escaped from the zoo. A piece of the *Tilbury's* keel was found in the basement of a house three hundred yards away, having fallen through the roof. The tragedy resulted in the Explosives Act of 1875. It is also commemorated, as every canal book hastens to tell, by the revised assembly of 'Blow Up Bridge'. When re-erected, the supporting pillars were reversed and the grooves worn by the earlier towlines may be seen on the backs of these supports.

Aboard the *Swan*, Richard Saunders, a friend of John's, was assembling a little shanty at the bow, in order to provide fit and proper accommodation for our chemical lavatory. The basis of this concoction was the forward cratch, the decorated triangular piece of wood at the front end, to which he had attached numerous baulks of substandard timber, the whole adopting a rudimentary tent-like form. Much of the wood had been purloined from a building site, with a wink and a nod from the foreman. Each plank, possessed as such pieces do, countless rusty nails, which were now being flattened willy-nilly. An expectant throng awaited a lavatory of unprecedented comfort.

In pre-war days, London's waterways were intensively active. Canal horses and tug at Bow in the 1930s

Their hopes were blasted when I managed to smite the final bridge before the Regents Canal Dock. The cratch and headlight just tipped the arch. Amidst mighty cheers from the *William*, our new bow shelter disintegrated, opening up like some speeded-up daffodil, the planks splaying in all directions. We moored in the dock, a monumental establishment with Lake Titicaca expanses, and to mollify our lavatorial engineer went to a pub in the Commercial Road.

We returned to find the fleet being marshalled for the tideway. Mooring warps the diameter of household washing lines were draped, as a gesture, around the bollards intended to restrain 3,000 ton ships. After an interminable wait, obligatory, in my experience, at all ship locks, the outer gates were opened to disgorge us into the Thames.

To say that we left like greyhounds from the trap is an exaggeration. Nevertheless, *Swan* was able to make her best speed up the river, in the region of six knots. We quickly passed a motorized punt, bravely facing into an awkward stumbling chop and one by one overhauled our fellow voyagers.

The sights of the Thames are familiar, and likeable; Tower Bridge, where once a London bus successfully jumped a widening gap between the bascules; big timber ships listing heavily as they wait to enter the Surrey Docks; the Tower itself. I once had ample opportunity to inspect the impressive river frontage when my brother and I sloshed sea wards in my canoe, in the teeth of a fresh easterly. Lightermen would run out to warn us off the clanging trots; worse still, mooring buoys the size of bungalows tore sideways towards us as they surged about in the ebb. That eventful journey ended in a grave strategic

The Pool of London, rarely this busy nowadays

On the tideway, with Cannon Street in the background, left

blunder. Having swallowed enough filthy river water to put us in quarantine for the rest of our lives, we decided to land at what proved to be the Northern Outfall Sewage Works. Here effluent from half the Home Counties is processed and we went aground right at the sewer mouth. Vivid memories flood back: scrambling through banks of filth, clutching pathetic belongings such as a chart and an apple; camping on the ornamental lawn; cleaning up. An impressive establishment, extensively automated, the Northern Outfall retained a personal touch. In the lavatory was a king size deodorising bottle, with the wick pulled right up.

Upstream of the Pool, are several impressive warehouses, and many less inspiring office blocks, particularly on the south side where a rampart-like row gazes bleakly across at a much more inspiring Vickers Tower. Pedestrians on the bridge became personages in a Lowry painting, occasionally pausing to gaze down at *Swan* from their exalted heights. John, who was steering, began to have difficulty with smuts again, and was compelled to adopt a low, racing posture at the tiller. Driftwood sped past and a flat iron, one of the colliers that serve Battersea Power Station, materialized, like some cloud of doom, in the air space beneath Lambeth Bridge.

At Hammersmith Pier, where we stopped to pick up more passengers, an attendant told us we were not wanted. It is one of the features of the Lower Thames that there are few places at which it is possible to moor a boat. A good spot would have been Festival Pier, now abandoned for want of use. Here, too, the main function of the incumbent was to inform passers-by that 'You can't bring that boat in here, mate'. The only effective stratagem was to arrive, with people making fast with ropes at the opposite end of the boat to wherever the argument took place.

Our guests told us how mottled we had become, the engine having surpassed itself, in conjunction with a brisk breeze. We journeyed on to Brentford, passing through a veritable plateau of driftwood while upon the Boat Race course, before we turned back into the canal system. Here the locks are electric and, in a pool above is the traditional transhipment point from barge to narrow boat. Photography is forbidden from the footbridge, presumably because it allows too penetrating a view into the boat peoples' cabins. On this occasion only two pairs of narrow boats were to be seen. As a sign of the times, one of the butties had sprouted a television aerial.

The *William* had rejoined us, to puff alongside up the locks past Hanwell Institution. A small boy ran down the towpath shouting some mysterious rallying cry; immediately three quarters of the crew disappeared. They had found a riding school. Children rode horses bareback, were scraped into hedges and risked their necks generally, as they had been doing all day. Dennis Jewiss hove into sight to roar at them and the sport summarily ceased.

At each lock the *William* and *Swan* would leave simultaneously, side by side. Whichever got ahead would always create a wave, sufficient to carry the other boat along. This was the secret of the horse-drawn passenger craft of earlier years; an initial effort by the horse would lift a boat onto the travelling wave which normally preceded it. The beast could then proceed at a trotting or even a galloping pace with relatively little expenditure of energy.

In our case, the phenomenon made it difficult for one boat to get ahead of the other. At lock number ninety, Norwood Top, a disgraceful thing happened. Neither boat would give way to the other and for roughly a mile we proceeded side by side at 4 mph. We made little wash, I hasten to add, for this is a great canal crime, as it undermines the banks and causes silting. Working boats often proceed for considerable distances 'breasted up', but I am sure that narrow boat racing is scarcely condoned by the authorities. We proceeded for some time in this manner, in an atmosphere of mutual banter. Occasionally, the boats would separate for a foot or so, then crash back together, amidst cries from those on washing-up fatigues.

At last, one of the boats, not ours, thank goodness, ran hard onto an unsuspected reef. Everyone on the roof fell over for the umpteenth time. Poles and boathooks were being called for in stentorian terms as we crept on back to Cowley, where, in the October mists, we finally moored.

Chapter 5

Up-Country Journey

Having blooded us at Stratford and at Limehouse, John buoyantly proposed a more exhaustive voyage for the following year. Winter flitted by in a series of engine dismantlements. Grotesque groaning sounds from the clutch had warned us that all was not well there; the bearing was found to be a mere rusty husk, containing four or five pitted and hexagonal steel balls. The cylinder head yielded little except some carbon, while the gargantuan and singularly inefficient silencer when unscrewed fell precipitately upon my foot. John painted the cabin sides red and annointed the tiller with spiralling stripes in the original canal manner, a style which had preceded the pop art era by some hundred years. We also erected a rudimentary deck across the back half of the hold.

John, Martin and myself were by no means the first to plan such a journey, although the fashion is a very recent one. Considering the dates at which the canals evolved, there was a depressingly long time lag before the lay citizen ventured upon them. The Victorians, doubtless obsessed with the Iron Horse, preferred not to think about canals too hard. Reginald Blunt who essayed a trip from Reading to Bath and back through the now defunct Wilts and Berks Canal, was, to my knowledge, the first person to launch himself upon such waters for pleasure.

Blunt published an account in *Pall Mall Magazine* for 1888. Apart from an equine white power unit named Methuselah, the trappings of his adventure had much in common with our own. He and his brother lived under canvas in the hold and there were even doubts that the *Ada* might prove 2 inches too wide for the already decrepit locks of the Wilts and Berks. There is also the following gem, a letter from a boatman:

> 'Sir i rite to you heari
> ng that you was going to have
> Mr. H-'s boat ada wich is not a bit
> of good for the wilts and berks canal as
> she is to wide and long to go along the
> men that is are going with you are no more
> fit to go with her than nobody as Mr. H-
> as not got a man a working for him that

Author at the 'elum. 'Swan' has a distinctive pointed back end.

> knows where you want to go
> to as the wilts and berks canal wa
> nt men who are accomston the canals
> as to working the locks are very dangerous
> and that for a donkey would never tow a
> boat like the ada as she tows so heavy sir
> rite and say wether you will want me.'

As Mr Blunt says, 'The moral of this was so clearly indicated in its last sentence that the rest did not greatly perturb me'.

For the remainder of this long and exhilarating account, I would refer readers to Inland Waterways Association *Bulletin 77* which is edited by Hugh McKnight and which I also recommend. I am indebted to this periodical for the above quotations.

Soon enough, I myself was asleep in the hold of a narrow boat; Martin and John were blowlamping and by the time I had lurched out of bed, we had cast off our moorings above Cowley Lock and were hammering northwards through Uxbridge at the start of our marathon.

The timber and canvas platform under which I slept was, in all respects except headroom, as good as many cabins. Sometimes, however, my head would make sharp and unsympathetic contact with one of the chains. On such occasions, as on this first morning, I would subside back into bed with a cackling cry, to be revived with coffee and the threat of missing something interesting in the world beyond the steel hull sides.

We passed through Watford's Cassiobury Park, which, on a summer's morning, is a delightful place, with the sun streaming through gaps in the overhanging trees and the canal winding between the woods in one right angle bend after another.

At night, Cassiobury is a very different spot. It is easy then, amongst mists and drooping branches, to imagine the great negro who could jump the 14 foot wide lock chamber. He would drop the paddles, cut ropes, close gates and generally terrorise the boatmen. The stories of this centuries-old character have appeared in several books and have also been scoffed at, presumably by people who have only been up the canal by daylight. The man was eventually slain by a boatman, reputedly with the tool he was forever stealing, the vital L-shaped windlass that is essential for working the locks. The story I like best is of the old tree which was felled in the park some years ago. It was found to be hollow and filled with rusty windlasses.

We pressed on for Tring summit, vying or abstaining, as our natures took us, for the privilege of riding the bike. In spots the path had been renewed with large egg-shaped stones so that it resembled a long shred of Brighton Beach and provided torturing territory for the pedal cyclist. A few yards of this were enough for most of us, but Martin, muttering vaguely about training for the rugby season, would bash on for mile after mile.

At Berkhampstead another crowd surrounded the lock, which on closer inspection was-found to contain two men, swimming. Polite early requests failed to coax them out and it took John's 'Get out or you'll be killed' to convince them of the danger. The sight of *Swan* bashing about, her big propeller whirling in the churning water, was, we hoped, sufficient vindication of our threats.

The summit level at Tring is through a narrow and wooded cutting with, at the far end, a splendid view across the reservoirs at Marsworth. The sun set across the water as we set our backs against the balance beams and London seemed a million miles away. We spent the night eight miles farther on, at Leighton Buzzard, then pressed on down to the long and winding pound north of Bletchley. In just under fifteen miles there is one lock, at

Cassiobury before the war. Barges of this type at one time travelled as far north as Berkhampstead, but rarely went beyond.

Fenny Stratford. Had the early surveys been accurate there would be no lock at all; in fact its presence is an accident and the canal drops at this point by about 6 inches.

Such long and undisturbed stretches enabled us to attend to the routine chores, such as cooking which Martin did willingly, John did well, and which I detested. Unhappily the Hostess had at last given up the unequal struggle with time and had broken in half. It was replaced by two calor gas rings on which we did all our cooking. Otherwise the interior still complied with the standard format of the working boats. John slept upon the cupboard

door-cum-bed, Martin upon the floor. We ate from a table which actually consisted of another hinged locker door, handsomely decorated in roses and castles.

The motor, being so awkward to restart, was kept running from dawn 'til dusk. Its constant vibration meant that a watchful eye had to be maintained over all plates and cups. At certain frequencies the table vibrated in sympathy and there was one dreadful slow running engine speed which we all tried to avoid. This sent heads oscillating upon necks and rendered the process of eating, and particularly biting, a most inexact science.

Our engine nonetheless made us several friends. Many of the canal people knew *Swan* from the days when she carried carbon bi-sulphide for Messrs Cowburn and Cowpar. Latterly she had been worked on the Bridgewater Canal by Gordon Waddington, carrying coal. Boatman after boatman would assure us that he had been one of *Swan's* few steerers. 'Used to be an acid boat,' they would say. 'Had two big tanks in her.' The next authority would snort with derision at the mention of tanks and emphatically assert that she carried carboys. 'Was he Tanks or Carboys?', we would ask one another after the latest encounter with an expert. Supporters of the tanks theory appeared to be winning, but there were sufficient 'carboys' about to make it an entertaining clash of philosophies. There were even a few outsiders, the canal equivalent of those who backed Marples as Tory leader. One very elderly man came out of his cottage to tell us that he had worked the *Swan* on the Severn from Gloucester. 'Bolinder', he exclaimed on hearing the engine note, and smiled nostalgically. 'She shakes a bit sometimes', and here, vibrating as we nodded from the bottom of the lock, we were forced to agree with him.

Since my first journey on the Grand Union, about ten years ago, commercial traffic had declined miserably. From time to time, however, we would meet loaded pairs, several of them already well known to us; the gay and colourful *Roger* and *Raymond* and the craft of Willow Wren Canal Transport Services. Many of these boats were chartered from the

Left: *A boatwoman of the late 19ᵗʰ century.*

Below: *Mrs Harris and baby Paul, boat people with the Willow Wren, mid-1960s*

otherwise disbanded British Waterways carrying fleet and gave every impression of being worked far harder under new management.

At Stoke Bruerne we met several working boats, deeply loaded. The first, a single motor boat operated by one man, was down through the lock in moments. Its engine, presumably with silencer removed, banged away as it was put into reverse at the bottom of the lock. A rope from the towing mast pulled the gate open and untied itself as the boat roared out. The boatman, seeing me take a photograph of this sensational scene and perhaps also

Stoke Bruerne in winter 1967, an uncharacteristic scene of the day, with almost the entire Willow Wren fleet waiting for the completion of repair work

Stoke Bruerne in mid-Summer 1967. Crowds at weekends are now a commonplace. The farthest building in the background, once a grain store, is now a museum

annoyed that I had brought *Swan* too near the bottom gate, blazed at me with an air rifle as his boat slid past ours. His remarks, shouted above the din, were fortunately unintelligible but were thought to include 'and don't send it to no magazine neither'. In deference to his wishes the two pictures taken, one of which, rather shakier than the other, includes the actual firing of the gun, have not been published. This incident can, I think, be taken as a reminder that the boat people have never liked being regarded as exhibits. The Water Gipsy image, quite an incorrect one incidentally, couldn't have been better calculated to make them smart.

In the lock above were a further pair, motor boat and butty, breasted up, and so deeply laden that they grounded on the bottom of the lock. The engine beat, like a motor cycle's but with a much sharper cracking note, once again obscured all comment. Why canal transport is popularly supposed to be lazy and gentle has always been a mystery to me. The explosive noise, the thrashing water, and the long dramatic shapes of the boats themselves make for a dynamic atmosphere which the film *The Bargee* totally failed to capture. Here the racket rose almost to the threshold of pain. I exchanged grins with the boatman as his pair dragged themselves through the shallow water, but I did not take his picture.

At the top of the Stoke Bruerne flight is the recently established and fascinating waterways museum. It has become a popular spot, far more so than in the days when it was a mere stopping place for working boats. Hereabouts the canal is extremely tidy, the buildings well cared for and the large bridge entirely painted white. John Sheldon feels that paint, its application and its consequences, are what British Waterways will best be remembered

Narrow boat of the type built for the Grand Union Company 1931

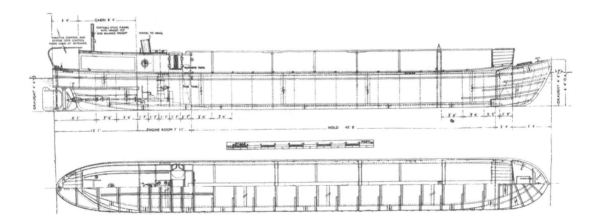

for. The blue and yellow livery had been cheerlessly applied to the working boats upon nationalization in contravention of tradition. Certainly the odd rashes of tidiness such as at Stoke Bruerne, contrasted jarringly with the many under-maintained stretches which were farther removed from the public gaze.

On the narrow canals at any rate, the British Waterways Board did little to expand the transport of goods by water. Rather, it consolidated the position of these waterways in their position at the bottom of the league, the Eeyore of the communications world.

The Observer at that time quoted a typical bit of official guff, emanating from a British Waterways official; 'But the Rhine goes to useful places. Our rivers are all in the wrong place. Where does the Thames go? Lechlade. And the Severn? Shrewsbury. If one of them only went to Birmingham we'd make a million.'

So many questions are begged here that it would take the rest of this book to enlarge upon them fully. Suffice to say that the continental waterways system, which flourishes, does not consist of the Rhine only, nor is it all as flat as Holland (or Lincolnshire). The Grand Union, however, *does* go to Birmingham and its locks are of comparable dimensions to the ones up to Lechlade. Were British Waterways, then, attempting to 'make a million'? We pushed on to Birmingham to see.

Chapter 6

Tunnelling to Brum

A voyage to Birmingham is not for the claustrophic. There are two massive tunnels on the Grand Union Canal, at Blisworth and at Braunston, with a 430-yarder at Shrewley, farther north, as a sort of postscript. None of them has a towpath and in the days of horse boats craft had to be legged through. Two men, or sometimes the boatman and his wife, would lie out on the boards rigged one each side of the bow and by walking along the tunnel wall would painfully drag the loaded boat forward.

At Blisworth Tunnel, just under two miles in length, professional leggers would do the job. They were paid one shilling and six pence a trip, were licensed, and wore armlets to distinguish them from the undesirable freelances. They worked in one direction only, twelve men in the northbound team and twelve southbound, with four from each gang on the nightshift. Fights and accidents were frequent; occasionally men went to sleep and fell from their legging boards and into the water. When a steam tug was introduced its crew perished from suffocation, and further ventilation shafts had to be dug.

The tunnel had taken so long to build that its opening was delayed until 1805, five years after the remainder of the canal; in the interim period Outram, the engineer in charge, constructed a tramway over the hill for the transhipment of goods. Since those early days the brick lining has given continual trouble and has cracked and leaked and slipped and fissured.

Blisworth, then, has a reputation, but it is none the less an exciting part of the journey north. Martin Johnson took the tiller as we entered. *Swan's* headlight was switched on and John and I hitched up our respective coat collars and crammed down our hats in readiness for the expected downpour from the roof.

Unlike Braunston Tunnel, where an early engineering blunder is commemorated by a kink near one end, Blisworth is dead straight. If no other boats have passed and the air is clear, you can sometimes see the entrance, a tiny speck which could easily be the headlight of an approaching boat. We blasted along, occasionally shrinking from the torrents of water from the ventilation shafts overhead and shouting above the engine noise. The scarred brickwork slipped past the arc of light while flakes from the roof were being walloped

Above: *Leggers emerging from the 3056 yard tunnel at Blisworth.*
Left: *Spoil heaps and ventilation shafts above the tunnel*

loose by the exhaust. Finally the other entrance, for so long a mere dot, expanded into a semi-circle of countryside, and after almost half an hour under the hill, *Swan* slipped out into a narrow cutting.

On such occasions everyone, for a few moments, resembles Funf the master spy, shrouded, compressed and furtive. A leering stalagmite at the stern turned out to be Martin who, in common with the cabin top, had been spattered with soot, water and brick chippings. With

Braunston yet to come, John immediately set about making a deflector for the exhaust chimney, to avoid any repetition of the trouble.

Beyond the cutting, the canal wanders through pleasing countryside, apart from a somewhat cheerless stretch beside the M1 Motorway. It was here, unhappily, that we lit upon a padlock around the gates of Buckby Bottom Lock and here we stuck for the night sandwiched between the noise of two more fortunate modes of transport. Buckby is an ironical place for the canal enthusiast as the main railway line from Euston also runs alongside. The Grand Union had, if anything, deteriorated since its opening 165 years previously. That narrow boats could still compete under such depressing circumstances and against such heavily subscribed rivals seemed to be an admirable testimony to the advantages of carriage by water.

John Sheldon is something of a curry connoisseur and also an expert chef. We locked ourselves down in the cabin and restored our good spirits with gigantic platefuls of excellent Indian food. Do the boatmen of Hooghly, I wonder, settle down to sausage and mash?

We were quick to enter the flight in the morning before anyone could overtake and leave us with the extra, and unwanted task of emptying each lock again before *Swan* could enter. The last boat through must have been heading in the opposite direction, for all the chambers were empty and we had an easy road. John's poor old bicycle was wilting under the strain of lock-wheeling and we were thankful not to use it. A slow but nonetheless accelerating puncture demanded repeated pumping, the brakes were not at their best and various wires would unwind themselves from the crossbar and attempt to snare any knee which happened to be passing. The bike was left in the hold.

Boats pulling open bottom gates at Long Buckby. The ropes are tied with slipknots and detach themselves from the rails as the pair moves out

Narrow boats pass in Braunston Tunnel

At the top of the flight is Norton, the junction with the branch from Leicester, a truly beautiful waterway down which we hoped to return in about ten days' time. It has narrow locks, only 7 feet wide as opposed to a 14 foot gauge on the main line. Once clear of the M1, which is passed just north of Watford Gap Service Station, there are no locks on the Leicester section for 20 miles and scarcely a village in that distance.

Braunston Tunnel provided few problems; the new deflector worked well although it was later flattened when someone cut a bridge a bit fine and shaved it against the arch. We shared the six locks below the tunnel with a hired cruiser, entering each chamber first and pinning *Swan* in forward gear against the bottom gate to avoid damage to the frailer craft alongside.

A stockade of working boats, lying outside the Willow Wren yard, reduced our progress from the bottom lock to the staid gait demanded at these gatherings. The chief fear engendered was one of scandal or rumour, for gossip can spread through the canal system with a rapidity I find astounding. News of misdemeanour travels fastest of all and reputations stand or fall at the drop of a paddle. A slow trip, a stranding, a parted rope; little goes unremarked. If you hit a bridge there's always someone waiting to come swinging around the bend, and transfix you with a beady gleam and an 'Owdyerdo avingabitoftroublethen?' before bashing away delightedly in order to tell everyone all about it.

Just beyond lay Michael Streat's abode, which, of course, we now knew rather well. The staff were probably steeling themselves at the sound of our approach, in anticipation of another noisy bout of scale chipping. 'What do they want?' we heard a nervous voice enquire over the intercom as *Swan* nosed around the turn. Fortunately we were in search of a mere seventy gallons of diesel fuel and had no intention of insinuating ourselves in order to use the place as a workshop once again. Blue Line Cruisers, Michael Streat's firm, contrives to be both benign and efficient. It has inherited the aura of earlier generations, for here are several docks where narrow boats used to be built and indeed amongst the ever-expanding pleasure craft activity, Blue Line still ran three pairs of narrow boats. Here too was once a transhipment depot where early steamers transhipped their cargoes and swapped butties, a complex piece of administration which stemmed from the existence at that time of narrow locks only, north of Braunston. A resident team of horses worked the butties along the remaining leg to Birmingham although, as everywhere on the canals, there were exceptions and complexities. The 'greasy ockers' worked steam-powered craft right through from London to Birmingham, with a regular crew on the steamer and the butty operated by a family. The steamers were based at Ocker Hill, Birmingham, hence the derisory nickname. They had large crews, while the sizeable engine occupied a certain amount of space which might otherwise be devoted to cargo. The fuel was coke, ten bags being the standard consumption for a trip from Southall to Braunston with a loaded butty. The steamers eventually gave way to the semi-diesel, although for several years, Fellows, Morton and Clayton, one of the largest carrying companies, jibbed at internal combustion

Below left: *Lock beam on the Grand Union near Marsworth.* Below right: *The Blue Line premises at Braunston. This was once a transhipment depot; in the background is the old boat building shed and beyond the cast iron bridge which carries the towpath alongside the Grand Union Main Line*

Above left: *One-time cargo transhipment crane at Braunston.* Above right: *Martin with one of the big worm driven paddles installed in the pre-war modernization programme*

because of the pervasive and contaminating nature of the fuel. The last steamer in service, the *Earl* was laid to rest in a backwater of the Oxford Canal in 1931.

Reluctantly, we left Braunston behind. Once again anxious fingers twiddled the speedwheel as *Swan* approached the blind bend at the little triangular junction. We took the left fork, continuing towards Birmingham along the so-called Main Line which hereabouts runs through the countryside almost eerily deserted.

Calcutt Locks loomed and it was here that we encountered two boy canoeists *en route* for Stratford-on-Avon. Having spent several holidays slapping and sploshing along canals myself and knowing what a dreadful bind it is to portage at the locks, we took them aboard. Some years ago in my old canoe *Stickleback* we met a loaded pair of working boats on a bend in the same stretch and were almost swamped in their wash. A weatherbeaten old crone in the butty cackled something about Rock n' Roll (then the great rage) as they swept by and we realized that in the rough and tumble of the canal world, canoes are very small fry indeed. They are not allowed to use the tunnels or locks and the alternative passage along the towpath demands the resource of a Colonel Fawcett and stoical resilience in the face of overwhelming brambles.

The remaining locks on the Grand Union were all reconstructed in the 1930s. Many canal authors have referred to the paddle gear which was then installed, usually in the most deferent terms. These sluices operate on a worm gear instead of the common toothed bar and cogwheel principle; they are nonetheless very hard to wind. If a lock was 'against' the boat (as most of them seemed to be), it had first to be filled, involving the raising of two paddles. Each one required, I think, twenty very heavy turns of the windlass. To drain the lock two more paddles had to be raised, by which time the operator had turned puce with exertion.

There are twenty-three locks on the descent to Warwick and beyond, at Hatton, twenty-one more, all in one flight. After these, the lighter paddles on the narrow canals are just toys in comparison. Perhaps toughest of all are the five locks at Knowle. These are incredibly hard work, with several paddles apparently being completely inoperable. John Sheldon,

Sunken boat in one of the old narrow lock chambers at Hatton, now in use as a spillway

a keen rowing man, bent his burly biceps to the task but frequently came off second best. Knowle locks would form excellent territory for some new Olympic event, or the eliminating heats of the Mr Universe contest.

Between these battlegrounds, the canal is most pleasant, apart from a short stretch through Leamington, which is sordid and quite unworthy of a spa. At Kingswood Junction, where the North Stratford Canal enters the Grand Union, we met one of the infrequent pairs of commercial craft. Motor boat *Bognor* with butty *Moon* in tow had run aground on the bank opposite the junction. As craft coming out of the Stratford have to cut over the inside of a bend they almost inevitably run on to the mud. It was encouraging to see that even the experts cannot avoid doing so, though disconcerting to note the ease with which they extricated themselves. This Willow Wren pair had brought timber up to Birmingham using the North Stratford in both directions, a route which a year or two previously had been quite unused by commercial traffic. I was told that the passage of loaded boats had somewhat improved its condition (from well-nigh impossible to marginal, I subsequently discovered).

Far from being a hub of commerce, Birmingham's waterways proved depressingly inert and the odd factory which acknowledged the canal as anything other than a refuse tip was a rarity indeed. Out of sight out of mind; far too many business organizations, let alone private citizens, were hurling their junk into the water. We began to run aground again, particularly under bridges. If I had to drive a motor car along a road littered with old bricks and biscuit tins I would feel understandably aggrieved. On the canal we had to contend with bicycles, mattresses, motor tyres, sand and barbed wire, yet none of the people who watched our poling and swearing efforts looked the slightest bit concerned.

However abused, Birmingham's canals have a certain fascination. We decided to visit Gas Street Basin, which sounds too good to be true and is in fact right in the heart of the city. To get there *Swan* had to pass down one flight of seven and up two flights of six and thirteen narrow locks. The canal winds under, around and through the factories. Look up, and there is the main line station, look left and you can see motor-cycles being made, or steel being cut. It is all as exciting as it's dirty, an intricate, many-faceted monument to the seeds of industry and to the growth of an urban jungle.

Chapter 7

The Road to Worcester Bar

Although Worcester Bar is smack in the middle of Birmingham, very few of the locals seemed to know where it was or what it referred to. It was here, in the basin off Gas Street, that, with great enterprise, a new carrying company had set up its HQ, at a time when Birmingham's canals had almost reached rock bottom in condition, navigability and civic interest. We decided to make a small detour, to visit the basin and investigate the situation there at first hand.

Accordingly *Swan* turned left at the T junction above Farmers Bridge locks. We bounced her round the acute angled bend, having climbed in total twenty locks since leaving the Grand Union. At some we had been jammed solid by debris wedged between the boat and lock walls. The Digbeth flight in particular had demanded much both in patience and muscle. Here the canal was littered with so much timber that we were tempted to walk on it. It only needs one such piece behind a lock gate to wedge a boat solidly; I beat savagely at the recalcitrant baulks with a long shaft while John and Martin rocked and swung *Swan* to get her free. As a reward to the diligent and the determined, there exists, at the top of these two flights, a wide and lockless stretch of water. This is the Main Line, backbone of the complex Birmingham system, and possessed of a fascinating nomenclature: Rough Hills, Horseley Fields, Deepfields, Blomfield, Pudding Green, and Watery Lane Junctions, the connections with the Old Main Loop, the Soho Branch, Spon Lane Locks Branch, Dunkirk Junction, the Oozells Street Branch and the two junctions with the Icknield Port Road Wharf Loop. There are many arms which are no longer navigable, some being completely obliterated.

Strangely enough Worcester Bar survives, a memory of a cold war which came to an end in 1815. When the Worcester and Birmingham Canal was mooted, the Birmingham Canal proprietors opposed the venture, feeling that it would divert traffic from their own waterways. They therefore refused to allow any physical connection between the two canals and for several years they were separated by a dam or quay, only the width of an average city pavement but across which all cargoes had to be transhipped. Eventually this time-wasting foolishness came to an end and a stop-lock was cut across one end of the Bar.

Now the Bar had been put to some use, for a line of working boats was moored stern-on to the quay. When we arrived, looking for a berth, all the good ones were occupied and

The spirit of Brum. Boats and smoke at Salford Bridge, where the Birmingham and Fazeley and the Tame Valley Canal meet the end of the Grand Union Main Line.

we made fast alongside the towpath. The species narrow boat, unconverted and still in working order, had become such a rarity in the Midlands that Sam Waller came over and asked us which company we represented. Sam proved to be a director of the Birmingham and Midland Canal Carrying Company which had been launched on money contributed by enthusiasts and chiefly with craft purchased when British Waterways disbanded its own carrying fleet.

When seen together, working boats can have an amazing variety of shapes and size. In this respect they are like cows, commonly assumed to be identical, although really running a wide gamut of character, shape and disposition. We moved *Swan* alongside the massive *Linda*, built in 1931 as the *Victoria*, and, with her high freeboard, intended for use on the Thames. John Anderson, *Linda's* steerer, told Martin that he had given up his council house and a well-paid job in a foundry to join the new company. 'I was born on a boat, the wife the same. When you've been brought up on the canal, you find you can't leave it all that easily.'

While in the basin we enquired about the current state of the Dudley Tunnel, which is linked with limestone mines, the complexity and dimensions of which recall the might of trolls. We learnt that it was closed, pending the finale to some sterling deeds by a preservation society. Even if barred from admission, we resolved to take a look, for it required only a very small detour from our projected route. The next morning we chugged out of Gas Street Basin, under the main road bridge which recalls a postcard of Holland, and out along the Main Line.

For a city canal this is very wide and has the luxury of a towpath on each side. Such an arrangement forestalled the complicated and sometimes dangerous passing over of towlines when two horseboats met. Birmingham, incidentally, was one of the last strongholds of the horse-drawn working boat and I was told that two were still operating (since my writing this the number has declined to one).

The Main Line was largely engineered by Thomas Telford and bears the well-known characteristics of that gentleman's art. Brindley's earlier canal has been wilting under the strain of a colossal traffic. Towlines would tangle while the horses themselves frequently fell into the water; boatmen fought for access to a short summit, to which water had to be painfully pumped from out of mine shafts. Telford swept these conditions away by driving his new canal in a seventy foot deep cutting through the old Smethwick Summit. His twin

Left: *Gas Street Basin.* Above: *Worcester Bar, Gas Street. Th*
boats are moored stern-on to the Bar itself. In earlier days th
basin here was much more extensive, with arms extendir
beyond where the fence now stands in the background

Remnants of the Newhall Branch from the top of Farmers Bridge. This quarter mile arm used to pass beneath the bridge in the background. Picture taken in 1969.

towpaths easily coped with the 200 boats that passed each day and his high bridges caused no bottlenecks. Viewed from the *Swan* these bridges seemed miles high, built for the carriage of toy vehicles and insect pedestrians. From one such arch a boy was swinging out on a length of rope. He dangled precariously above the water before, spiderlike, he swung back to a footing on the embankment.

Canals and children go together in Birmingham, despite some determined efforts by authority to keep them apart. Any boat passing through will soon be trailing a nomadic crocodile down the towpath. Little boys will cry for rides and will trot alongside for hours, until one quite despairs of their ever seeing their homes again.

At Albert Junction we turned off to make towards Dudley and entered the short Gower Branch Canal. John's bashed-up old trumpet was deployed in its customary role of warning hooter and we locked up the flight of three to the Old Main Loop Line. 'OostheKennyBoorl?' the children demanded as they lined up like starlings on the balance beams 'Giussablowmister'. We gave them a blow, a cracked and rasping B flat. Martin looked at the grisly water and muttered 'Not that we'd expect to meet anything here', and a loaded Thomas Clayton boat came round the corner.

It is one of the phenomena of the inland waterways that you can go for hours without meeting another boat, then will encounter one on the sharpest and nastiest bend in the system. We gave this one the outside of the curve, for it was deeply laden, and noted the slow pumping note of the Bolinder engine as it passed. Thomas Clayton's boats were based at Oldbury. They were all decked in and worked as tankers, carrying liquid tar products from gasworks; because of this boat people called them gas boats. They once worked widely through the canal system and I can remember, some years ago, meeting many of these craft on the Shropshire Union as they plied between Birmingham and Ellesmere Port. They were all named after rivers: the *Lark*, the *Tweed*, the *Hebble*, the *Ohio* and many more. The boat we met was the *Umea*, one of three remaining from what was once a big fleet. It worked between gasworks in the Birmingham and Wolverhampton area until, shortly after our visit, the Clayton boatyard ceased business in order to make way for the construction of a motorway.

Mile by mile the Birmingham network has shrunk. Many canals have been closed because of the difficulties caused by subsidence and on the grounds that they are no longer used (which was rarely surprising, in view of their condition). This has happened in the Dudley area, as elsewhere, and our attempt to approach via the Tipton Green and Toll End Communication had been thwarted by virtue of its obliteration. Although the parallel

Ex-Thomas Clayton 'gas boat' Tay, *now in private hands, and maintained in its original condition with red livery and decked in hold*

Dudley Tunnel itself has a minimum headroom of only 5 feet 9 inches in bore, at nearby Netherton it is as big as many railway tunnels. It has a towpath on either side and we were able to look down into its black and gaping entrance from the aqueduct by which we crossed the Netherton Branch. Both this and the Dudley Tunnel are over three thousand yards long, although Dudley opens out into short cavernous cuttings at its northern end. Being closed, pending the attentions of the Preservation Society, we had to reach it by foot.

The last working boat went through in 1950 or thereabouts. We were amazed to see how clear the water now is, and how shallow. At the northern entrance a formidable bar had been created by the local kids, who had infuriatingly tipped the brick parapet into the water. Alongside stood the remains of another brick arch, bored into the bank and apparently curving upwards. I attempted to find its outlet from above and was nearly mown down by a goods train for my pains, for a railway crosses the entrance at the top of a steep and brambly embankment.

A member of the Preservation Society called by on a routine check against hooliganism and told us about the additional arch. Apparently, in the tunnel's early days, tub boats brought limestone from the mines within and were then shunted into a short branch tunnel, the remains of which we had observed. The cargo was then hoisted up a shaft and tipped into kilns built alongside the canal. The shaft was covered over many years ago, when the railway was built above it.

From this point to the end of the Main Line is about seven miles and a pretty depressing stretch it proved. *Swan* ground on, stirring up black clouds in the water as we penetrated Wolverhampton. It was late afternoon before we reached the twenty-one locks down to the Staffordshire and Worcestershire Canal and, subsequently, the Shropshire Union.

I went ahead to wheel the flight, for all the locks were empty and against us. It gradually became apparent that we were following another and slower boat; this turned out to be a pleasure cruiser which itself had no locks in its favour. The husband of the middle-aged couple aboard was doing all the work and would dash down to the next lock, set to fill, then return several hundred yards to recover his boat from the lock he was allowing to drain.

Efficient lock working is a simple exercise in logistics which many pleasure craft owners are apparently incapable of fathoming. Despite often massive crews and a formidable total IQ it takes them an age to move through a flight with long, and wasted, periods when the boat is not moving forward and no water is entering or leaving the lock. The chap on this particular boat was, under the circumstances, managing admirably and deploying his time to best advantage. Since, however, he was only flesh and blood, the continued sprint up and down the path, the cranking of paddles and the jumping aboard were beginning to take their toll. John's bicycle was therefore coerced into the scheme. I would ride on, prepare the lock ahead of the first boat, and, if time, the one beyond. I then had to pedal madly back to refill each lock after craft one had left, in order to allow craft two to enter. In this way both boats arrived at the bottom in reasonable time, although I was beginning to emulate the bicycle in condition and travel weariness.

The Wolverhampton flight starts beside the engine sheds and finishes in the countryside at Aldersley Junction. From there it is but another half mile to Autherley Stop Lock and

Stonework detail, Wolverhampton Locks. The date obviously commemorates rebuilding of the chamber, the flight itself being constructed earlier

The bottom of the Wolverhampton Flight. Two canal cottages used to stand here at either side of the entrance. Both have now been demolished and the wrought iron lamp too has since disappeared

the Shropshire Union Canal. Fresh from the fray of the Main Line, and heartily glad to be in healthy surroundings again, we proceeded, with great gusto, to run aground three times before a large and appreciative audience of pleasure craft owners. 'What's the matter with them? It isn't all that difficult', remarked one onlooker, staring at *Swan's* wavering course in a perfectly straightforward channel. In point of fact, the dreaded zig-zags, once begun, are hideously difficult to diminish, as the boat loses all responsiveness when upon the bottom. Occasionally, a towpath, a bridge abutment or, worst of all, another boat will intervene to interrupt the progression. With these fears in mind, Martin strove valiantly at the helm, while a shrewd jab or two with the shaft brought *Swan* back on the straight and narrow. Finally recovering our faculties we moved through the stop lock, past the many boats and members of Autherley Boat Club and in the dusk headed north once again, up the Shropshire Union Canal.

Chapter 8

The Shroppie

It grew dark as we moved up the Shropshire Union. The wind licked across the fields, and branches waved into the scope of the headlight. Soon the countryside began to roll. I think that evening is the finest, certainly the most mysterious, time to enter this canal, although some of its cuttings are so deep that they are always twilit and spooky. Clouds dashed overhead; the moon was up and at each bridge I half-expected to see a highwayman. Instead we met the *William* again.

She was returning from an exploration of the fastnesses of Merseyside, with a complement of Beauchampions. The oncomer was first discernible only by the orb of light up the canal ahead although soon, above the wind, we could distinguish schoolboy voices of command and counter instruction. They flashed their headlight, we flashed ours. They stopped, we stopped, then, finally, I opened up the engine and steered through the bridge, recognizing the *William* as we passed and enquiring after Dennis Jewiss whom it transpired was not aboard.

Unhappily our departure left the *William* rather high and slightly dry in the shallows, 'banked' as the canal people say. We did not think too much of it at the time, as *Swan* is not infrequently banked herself, an irritation rather than a catastrophe and one to be overcome by the deployment of various cunning ruses.

Dennis Jewiss, who had to tramp up the towpath from Autherley to locate his charges, afterwards told me that their engine had stalled and all the lights fused. 'Just wait 'til I catch up with them', he told his crew, 'And now', he said, eyeing me in his office some weeks later 'I have'. Whatever fate he intended he did not bestow, other than a guilty feeling that we should have stopped to snatch the *William* off the mud. Such a thought, I must confess, did not enter my head until we were well beyond the scene of the crime.

We spent the night in one of the cuttings, at Brewood (pronounced Brood), and in a dramatic photo-finish just made the pub by closing time. The presence of three unkempt strangers, coincident with the news that some terrorist had, within the last few minutes, smashed the lavatory, induced a faint air of hostility which marred an otherwise pleasant occasion.

Characteristic deep cutting near Tyrley, on the Shropshire Union, with Swan *characteristically aground on a small land slip*

Under a gathering cloud of suspicion we returned down the bank to the boat. From my bunk in the hold that night I could look out at the shadowy trees and the high skyline on either side of the cut. Wolverhampton engine sheds were just six miles back down the canal.

The next morning we passed on through the sparkling countryside. Martin fried some bacon while John checked the health of our patient Gardner which was still dhonking away as reliably as ever. Liley, who had been repairing a childhood omission by reading Winnie-the-Pooh, leaned on the tiller, hummed a little hum and sniffed the air in anticipation of breakfast.

We crossed, by aqueduct, Watling Street, a route as direct as our own. The Shropshire Union Main Line is distinctive for its straightness. Of all canals, it comes closest to Romanesque surveying, although it was one of the last to be built in Britain's canal era. It was also the last work of a very great engineer, Thomas Telford, and was not, in fact, opened until six months after he died.

The Birmingham and Liverpool Junction as it was first called, almost took the directest route across the Midlands countryside. Almost, but not quite, for at Shelmore Wood the line had to be diverted at the insistence of Lord Anson, who kept pheasants thereabouts and did not want them disturbed. William Provis, Telford's lieutenant in that sector, could doubtless have personally wrung every neck on the Anson estate, including that of the noble lord himself. The great embankment which by-passed the wood brought endless

Shelmore Embankment. The farmers still find the remnants of barrows and shovels in the fields below

trouble. It continually settled and slipped; hundreds of men fought to build up the soil, only to watch it continually subside. In one single slip, in August 1832, three years after the work began, a portion of the embankment 800 yards long, and half its width at the top, crashed into the muddy fields below.

Telford, old now and frequently ill, gave way to a younger man whose zest and confidence were almost crushed by the events at Shelmore. His name was William Cubitt, later to be chief engineer of the South-Eastern Railway. Finally he won and, albeit in a narrow and distinctly wonky channel, the first loaded boat passed through on March 2, 1835. Shelmore embankment had taken six years to build. From time to time local farmers still unearth bits of barrow and tools in the fields alongside.

In a chapter entitled 'The Last Canal', L. T. C. Rolt describes in greater detail the struggle at Shelmore, a battle won without mechanical aids, by men with picks and shovels who scarred the land to build a trunk waterway. Rolt's excellent biography *Thomas Telford* should also be referred to for the stories of the crumbling cuttings at Woodseaves, Grub Street and Cowley, where the projected 2,070 foot tunnel proved so unstable that it had to be reduced to a mere eighty-one yards.

Shelmore causes little trouble now, and like thousands before us we slipped over it with scarcely a thought for the struggles of its construction. It was on this embankment that we encountered a beautiful green narrow boat, the *Iona*, loaded with boy scouts and hauled by a towering horse called Jim. Jim and his much smaller companion Billy Budd resided at Norbury Junction, a small canal settlement which had become the base of a holiday hire

Below left: *Horse boat* Iona, *with traditional turk's heads and horse's tail decoration. The tiller has been reversed in its socket, to avoid accident to anyone emerging from the cabin. This is the time-honoured indication that a boat has stopped working for the day and may be passed by.* Right: *Norbury Junction in winter; British Waterways maintenance boat in full cry*

company. Harold Arnold, who worked there, came out to look at *Swan* and took us to his cottage to show us his many photos of our boat, taken when she was still in trade. Harry proved to be something of a pundit on canal boat decoration and a great horse boat enthusiast. He told me how Jim used to work in Birmingham on the dayboats there and how he (Jim) was so strong that he would stride away down the towpath scarcely aware, as he took up the slack, that he had a boat behind him. The other horse, Billy Budd, was much more characteristic of the standard canal animal. Such beasts required special training if they are not to leave chaos and consternation in their wake and most horses were trained to stand leaning into the halter to get a loaded boat moving out of a lock; even more important, they had to be taught when to stop.

A derelict canal, the Newport Branch, ran west from Norbury. Martin and I walked down to inspect the locks which, although minus all gates and machinery, at least had walls in fair condition. Efforts were at that time being made to form a lobby for their restoration for the Newtown Arm like its northern neighbour, the tragically abandoned Montgomeryshire Canal, would certainly have made an attractive holiday waterway. The Arm once linked with a network of tub-boat canals in the Shropshire coalfield. Great inclined planes were used for hauling small tub-boats up to a higher level. There were also locks with vertically lifting guillotine gates, 'Gullertynes' or 'Gallantines' in boatman's parlance.

Swan moved on to the great cutting just south of the Tyrley locks. Here the canal narrows as it passes through a short tract of jungle. There are frequent landslips at this point and onto one of these we duly ran for the customary half hour or so, before zestful poling allowed an escape.

At Tyrley there are five locks which plunge the canal down into another leafy canyon. The flight of fifteen beyond at Audlem are in more open territory, for here we were entering Cheshire, a less grand but, notwithstanding, pleasant county.

The following day we towed another narrow boat, the ex-British Waterways *Avon*. Her young owner had been painfully inching her from Haywood Junction, where he had acquired her, to Chester, where he lived and where he hoped to restore his craft. I wished him luck, for the *Avon* was in woeful condition, having been sunk for some time. She was minus her original Bolinder engine and had been progressing by means of a small outboard which proved quite useless in the strong cross-wind.

Our tow to Barbridge put a welcome spurt into the *Avon's* progress, although we all had a harassing time at Hurleston, where the Llangollen Arm runs off. I had nipped ashore to take some pictures and in being recovered, caused both boats to be blown hard into the

Thomas Telford's iron aqueduct at Longdon-upon-Tern, near Newport, on the now derelict arm from Norbury

Warehouses at Wappenshall, where the arm from Norbury joined a tub boat canal to the inclined plane at Trench

Iona in the Grub Street Cutting just north of Norbury. Progress in a horse-boat can be absolutely silent and, depending on the mood of the animal, surprisingly swift

bank opposite the junction. Several fishermen were summarily evicted as a result; we eventually took our leave in an atmosphere of withering distaste, slipped our tow at the junction and headed along the ten mile connecting arm to Middlewich and the Trent and Mersey canal.

There were few incidents at this stage of the trip. We met party after party of girls, newly embarked in hired British Waterways pleasure boats but regrettably heading in the opposite direction. In a rainstorm we also ran out of fuel, having forgotten to pump up the header tank. Ensconced in the engine-room, we bled off sundry airlocks and finally restored the Gardner to working order. By evening the *Swan* had reached Middlewich, a small town in the centre of the Cheshire salt-workings. This was as far north as we intended to go. We swung round the tight turn into a new canal, the Trent and Mersey, and headed south for the first time since leaving Uxbridge. Ahead was a slogging climb through thirty-one locks to Kidsgrove. Beyond that lay the forbidding hell-hole of Harecastle Tunnel.

Below left: *Grooved abutment near Market Drayton.* Right: *The* Avon *under tow*

Chapter 9

Two Hours in the Dark

When the canal traveller has finally scaled the thirty-one locks between Middlewich and Hardings Wood, he has, so to speak, climbed the beanstalk. Like Jack, however, he still has an uneasy feeling on reaching the top, the ogre in this instance being the tunnel under Harecastle Hill.

The problem is to get through the tunnel without too much damage to man or boat. The hazards are:
1. A subsiding roof, low enough in places to raze the cabin of many a pleasure boat.
2. A towpath, cantilevered out from one wall, an unreliable walkway with many pitfalls (at several points it has disappeared).
3. No ventilation shafts - a fanhouse at the southern end sucks air through during the week, but not at weekends.
4. Insufficient width for boats to pass.
5. A ghost.

Because of 1, boats take an age to get through the tunnel (it is 2,919 yards in length), while 4 demands the operation of a one-way system and the prospect of long delays. The record for incarceration is, I am told, held by the converted narrow boat *Stirling Castle*, which once stuck inside for four days. Factors 2, 3 and 5 contribute to the aura but affect only a minority of navigators.

With all these prospects on mind, the three of us embarked on the arduous business of locking *Swan* up from the Cheshire Plain to Kidsgrove, where the northern portal of the tunnel lies, just six miles north of Stoke-on- Trent.

From Middlewich, the canal lay parallel to the road, allowing us to exchange Sunday morning stares with the passing motorists. It was one of our rare confrontations with life beyond the canal bank, although we ourselves had been afloat for only a week. For a variety of reasons (laziness in my case) we had decided to grow beards. These had now reached a stage which get the wearers thrown out of restaurants and win them few admirers.

There are several salt works south of Middlewich, each emblazoned with a well-known slogan. Because this local industry involves pumping out an often essential strata of the earth's crust, this is a great area for subsidence. From time to time pictures appear in the local newspapers of houses tipped at crazy angles. Sometimes the canal settles too, and the embankments have often been built up, and in some cases re-routed.

The canal winds a lot. James Brindley built it for Josiah Wedgwood and thus allowed the Potteries to develop. Brindley's engineering technique was to follow contours as much as possible, mainly to economize on earth-moving. In consequence his bends were sharp. Inevitably, at one of the sharpest, we met a loaded working boat, the *Mendip*, closely followed by another, *Perch*. Both were carrying coal, a customary return load from Stoke. The early morning fishermen wound in their lines as a total of 210 feet of boat slid by.

In the north-west most of the locks take one boat only, rather than a pair, but on this particular stretch many of the locks were duplicated with two chambers standing side by side and a few yards apart. The two boats we met, being so close together, had obviously worked through the last pair of locks simultaneously.

Because of subsidence troubles, some lock walls had bulged and frequently only one lock in each pair remained operable. Dog-eared gates, wooden props across the chamber and mossy walls were often sufficient to warn us away from the derelict side, although on two occasions I blithely steered into the wrong entrance and was forced to back out ignominiously. Eventually I twigged the symbol for a lock out of order - a red circle painted on the abutment.

Thurlwood, a small village halfway up the ascent, has the distinction of a steel lock. This is one of the few modern innovations on the Trent and Mersey, a great cross-braced affair which has been devised to obviate settling. It has guillotine gates which also serve as sluices to let the water in or out. It is also beset with warnings against raising these gates too rapidly and presumably despatching a tidal wave down the canal.

While the lock was filling, Martin shot off in search of sorely needed supplies, finding, as so often in the small Cheshire villages, that there was a shop, not officially open on Sundays but giving service through the back door.

In wobbly fashion I preceded the boat by bicycle up the remaining flights. At one lock I had to outface the wheeler from a small cruiser coming in the opposite direction. He wished to refill the lock I had just emptied. This would have wasted valuable water and, on the old established principle of being there first, I stood my ground; *Swan* was, in fact, just leaving the previous lock and arrived roughly two minutes after the confrontation. Fortunately canals have entered a gentler era, at least at towpath level, and my meeting with the other wheeler was bloodless.

Steel Lock, Thurlwood, built to combat salt subsidence, although a conventional brick-built lock remains alongside

The Cheshire Locks. A red circle denotes that the right hand chamber is out of use

At this point the Macclesfield Canal crosses over by aqueduct, before making an unexpected junction with the west bank of the Trent and Mersey. As Robert Aickman says in *Know Your Waterways*, 'much time has been wasted in looking for an entry on the other and obvious side'. The final locks are known as the Red Bull Flight, taking their name from the adjacent inn, at which Thomas Telford once stayed whilst surveying the second Harecastle Tunnel. At the top, three working boats were moored, all facing south and loaded with felspar for the Potteries. I recognized Colin Harris, one of the children aboard, from photographs Hugh McKnight had sent to me some time before. A lively squib in a wolf cub cap, Colin leaped aboard *Swan*, seized the controls and started battering her at the top gate in order to leave at the first possible instant. Smoke shot from the exhaust chimney and brought John hurrying back from refilling our painted water bucket. With his nose just about level with the cabin slide, Colin informed us that he could 'drive anything - on the canal that is; he was gently but firmly dissuaded from driving *Swan* any further.

George Page who was once steerer of the *Swan*, came over from his boat *Trout*. Like the rest, he was waiting until the following day before entering the tunnel. As it was Sunday, Harecastle was officially open to northbound traffic only. Those who, like ourselves, wished to go south entered 'at their own risk', a phrase obscure in meaning but with ominous overtones. The working boats were all waiting until the timetable would again be in their favour and when, presumably, they entered at someone else's risk. As we could ill afford such a delay, we decided to chance the passage. George Page gave me the phone number of the tunnel keeper, who resided down at Chatterley at the southern end. I went off in search of a telephone, to inquire about going through against the system.

I found the northern end a macabre spot, overshadowed by a railway bridge which enclosed a small bowl in the land. Here the water is always bright orange, while two tunnel entrances stand picked out in whitewash against the hillside. There are in fact three tunnels at Harecastle, two for the canal and one the railway. James Brindley's tunnel, now closed, was the first ever major work of this kind other than mineshafts; Thomas Telford's tunnel, which superseded it, is the one now in use. The railway tunnel crosses both in the middle of the hill and is, in part, responsible for their collapsed condition. There was a certain irony in the reply I extracted from the pocket of railway porters I flushed from an office in Kidsgrove Station. 'Canal Tunnel? Nothing to do with us is it?' They despatched me to a distant call-box in the town.

The tunnel keeper proved no more helpful, being unable to give us any prophecy about when another boat might approach from his end; I gathered there was none inside at the moment. 'What happens if we meet someone in the middle?'
'Well it all depends who you meet, doesn't it?'
We decided to risk it and go in.

As a prelude, the three of us marched up to the entrance of Brindley's old tunnel and peered inside; we found it silted up to water level. It was first opened in 1777, five years after Brindley died and after eleven years' continuous work. Boats were legged through on a one-way system, with large fleets accumulating at each end, the crews mutinously waiting their turn. Within the tunnel other shafts ran into the workings of Golden Hill Colliery. The miners showed a distressing tendency to break through into the branches wherever it took their fancy, clogging the workings with spoil. In 1820 John Rennie, called in to inspect the tunnel, found the walls to be half worn through, found mortar so soft that bricks could be pulled out by hand and estimated the headroom to be only 6 feet in places.

As a result of this survey, Telford was called in to build another tunnel parallel to the old one. This took only three years to finish. The contractors, Pritchard and Hoof, of King's

Harecastle; Brindley's old tunnel is on the right

Norton, worked from the bottom of fifteen vertical shafts sunk into the hill. Incredibly, not a single life was lost.

Once again I am indebted to L. T. C. Rolt's biography *Thomas Telford* for these details. Once again I would direct readers to that work for a fuller and truly vivid account of one of the most successful engineering operations ever conducted.

For eighty-eight years the two tunnels were both used on a one-way system. Harry Arnold gave me the following figures quoted from George Westall's book *Inland Cruising*, published in 1908:

> Old Tunnel: Width at water level 8 feet 6 inches; height from water level 5 feet 10 inches.
> New Tunnel: Width at water level 9 feet 2 inches; height from water level 8 feet 10 inches.
> Traffic (both tunnels): 14 to 15 boats an hour; 12 hours a day.

Until quite recently an electric tug towed all boats through, picking up current from a cable above and hauling itself along another cable on the bed of the canal. When the roof sank even lower the system was abandoned and a fanhouse constructed at the southern end to suck out the fumes. The vertical shafts employed in the initial construction were unhappily temporary in nature and suffocation, therefore, has always been one of the hazards of Harecastle.

The Harecastle Ghost, according to Rolt, is called Kit Crew. It is said to appear at the intersection known as the Turnrail where the branch runs across to Golden Hill Colliery. When, in 1955, I canoed south through Harecastle, the thought of a meeting with Kit Crew added considerable sap to my sinews although then, as now, I saw no sign of the branch workings.

Rolt gives no information on the origin of the ghost's name nor to the similarity with the spectre of Crick Tunnel, which is known as Kit Crewbucket. We were, however, sped on our way by two incidental pieces of information.

'You go in without the fans on an' you'll be blinded. Come in tomorrow - after us', (Colin Harris).

'You go in there and Kidsgrove Bucket'll get you', (small boy on the towpath, speaking from behind a large toffee apple).

Is Kit Crew then, a corruption of Kidsgrove? No book I have looked at has been able to help, while, despite cross-examination, the young bystander could volunteer no information on when he first heard the expression.

In defiance of the apparition, Martin elected to walk ahead of *Swan* along the towpath, armed with a torch and a trumpet, on which to blow warning messages. With John steering and myself standing in the hold behind our bow shelter, *Swan* entered. At first it seemed a fairly normal tunnel, with sufficient clearance to keep a speed of about two miles an hour. This can seem quite fast enough, when the brickwork is slipping through the headlight arc and just skimming the corners of the cabin top.

Before long, however, the roof dropped in a series of alarming bulges. The clearance of the corners of our bow shelter and cabin gradually diminished to millimetres. John, by now of Colin Harris proportions as he shrank away from the low roof, cut down speed to a crawl. His existence at this stage was a far from happy one; he could scarcely see above the cabin top, while he was receiving the full brunt of the Gardner's exhaust.

Sometimes the roof dropped in a series of steps and occasionally the towpath had either been cut or worn away by boats keeping as far as possible from the opposite wall. At these points Martin hopped aboard and helped me push against the all-too-close brickwork.

Entering Harecastle. When Swan *reached the middle the roof barely cleared the klaxon seen silhouetted alongside the steerer*

Finally the inevitable happened and the steel forward bulkhead of the engine room struck an overhanging ledge. With a great bang *Swan* decelerated from 1 mph to dead stop in zero time. Unable to ascertain the damage, we just had to press on, *Swan* fitting the tunnel like a train in the London Underground but without any rails to guide her. Before this point, the lowest in the tunnel, a wooden loading gauge had been fixed to the roof. As all boats had to clear this, I would have thought the northern entrance a better place to put it.

After an age of edging progress, the engine's *pertunk pertunk* echoing in our ears, the roof began to lift again. We sighted a light ahead; I insisted that this was the other entrance but gradually, with a horrible sinking feeling, agreed with the others that it was a boat coming the other way and before which, technically speaking, we would have to back out.

The Sue June *at Harecastle. Beyond, the crew of* Swan *examine the damage*

It was a claustrophobic moment. I only hoped we were not up against an intractable working boat and that we could persuade her to reverse (we had already agreed upon a modicum of bribery for such a situation).

Finally we halted and confronted a small pontoon conversion, the *Sue June*. A diplomatic discussion took place on the towpath, hastened by the rising fumes from our engine. Finally our argument prevailed that, although technically in the wrong, it would take us hours to back out and we might all be gassed in the process. The southern portal on the other hand was plainly visible, a mere quarter of a mile away. Despite this the opposing crew were firmly convinced that they'd negotiated nine tenths of the tunnel already, a belief that considerably extended our negotiations.

The *Sue June* had only a small outboard and no reverse gear, so Martin and I helped push her out by heaving on the towpath rail, where it existed, *Swan's* bow and headlight looming up above us, and it was thus that we finally made the other end. As a final irony John's hat was swept off into the orange water by an immaculate, and accurate, steel height gauge.

We thanked the two men aboard the *Sue June* as their boat puttered once again towards the entrance, wishing them a safe passage. As far as we were concerned they richly deserved it.

The three of us took stock. John's hat had been recovered and had now taken on that patina which speaks of great experience. The cabin top showed several splits and started fastenings, although luckily most of the shock of impact had been absorbed by the springy steel roof above the engine room doors. We formed some unprintable opinions about the state of the waterway and vented them upon the tunnel keeper's dog which had greeted us with an unwelcome display of savagery. Ruefully we poled *Swan* off the bank.

Chapter 10

Down to the Trent

Over Stoke-on- Trent, the night sky crackles and glows. By the canalside practically every aspect of heavy industry is represented. There are collieries, a locomotive roundhouse of the American type, many potteries, of course, and an ironworks at the water's edge. Here the *Swan,* having struck up a close relationship with a polythene bag, some post office string and all the associated debris of a first class snarl-up, ground to a gentle halt.

Our only boathook was a caber-like timber shaft, about fifteen feet long. Taking turns with this, we would tug and jab at the mess around the propeller whilst, alongside, a mobile ladle was depositing red hot slag in open pits.

A carpet, no longer aesthetically acceptable, but still showing great strength and durability, was the first exhibit to be wrested from the deep. Other items followed, until we could proceed once more, past the kilns, the factories, and the derelict acreages, and towards Etruria. There were a number of wharves by the canalside, all of them unused although working boats still carried felspar to a point further south. At one factory a faded notice proclaimed enigmatically that 'Walking is Forbidden'.

Etruria Summit Lock has the distinction of a timber awning, so that it is, in effect, in an open-ended shed. This presumably dates from its days as a toll office. Here each working boat was measured with a special draught stick at four points. From these readings, the tonnage carried could be calculated and the appropriate toll levied. This system, reminiscent of tumbrils, beadles and town criers, had surprisingly persisted into the atomic age; in fact it was the severity and the many vagaries and awkwardnesses of the toll system that hastened the decline of the narrow canals. Other factors, of course, were the lack of modernization or even maintenance, together with a hostile management which merged into the obsessive negativism of the post-nationalization administrations. In 1963, the British Waterways Board did extend an annual licensing system instead, although this applied to certain areas only and the periods for which it was offered were far too grudging to encourage further investment on the scale the system needed.

At Etruria there is also the junction with the Caldon Branch, up which I once canoed. My most vivid memories are of some striking scenery and vast quantities of rain; I was also attacked by a swan. The Caldon Branch, which ran seventeen miles to Froghall and once

Canal, kids and steelworks, Stoke-on-Trent

Wharf of the Mersey Weaver Company, Stoke. The white piles are of felspar, one of the last traffics into the city by inland waterway

Covered lock, Etruria, once a gauging lock, where boats were measured for tonnage and tolls levied on cargo

even reached Uttoxeter, also has a short branch to Leek. Near here is Rudyard Lake, unexpectedly large and picturesque, which was built as a canal reservoir and after which (an oft-quoted story this) Rudyard Kipling was christened. Leek Basin no longer exists, having been 'modernized into a rubbish tip', as Robert Aickman so eloquently puts it.

Swan pushed on into the night, seeking to escape the fascinating but undeniably grim surroundings of the Potteries. Flashes of lightning lit our way and suddenly the rain was coming down like stair rods. John Sheldon, caught at the tiller, donned his gas inspector's cape while his lily-livered crew took refuge in the cabin. Fortunately open countryside reappears remarkably quickly beyond the city centre and we were soon able to moor up. At the lowest bridge yet encountered, steel rivet heads brushed against our forward shelter while simultaneously, John and Martin, beer fetishists both, spotted a pub that we could just reach before closing time.

The next day's journey, to a point near Fradley, thirty miles away, took us down into the valley of the Trent. En route I contrived to fall in at Barlaston, only up to the waist but with sufficient gusto to amuse a little girl on the hire cruiser moored next to us.

The scenery here is gentle and most attractive. The only industrial intrusion is the small township of Stone, from which incidentally, I first started boating, on the cruiser *Angela*, hired from the Canal Cruising Company.

An everyday scene. John clears the prop with the shaft

Ten miles beyond is Great Haywood, the junction with the Staffordshire and Worcestershire Canal. Here we turned off for a mile to investigate 'The Wide'. This is a lake-like pool in the canal, overlooked by a folly on the hill and faced across the valley by the wooded hills of Cannock Chase. Nearby stands one of Brindley's characteristic aqueducts over the River Sow, with, farther south and on the Trent and Mersey again, another across the Trent itself. These could be more accurately described as embankments pierced by shallow culverts.

The Wide itself is popularly believed to have been the spot at which Izaak Walton served his apprenticeship; presumably therefore it existed as an ornamental lake in the grounds of Tixall Hall, long before the canal was built. I spent a holiday there once, in a houseboat which had previously been an inspection craft for the directors of the Trent and Mersey and which had undeniably seen better days. It was an atmospheric vacation, one of frosts and mists. Our abode had cut glass windows, together with many trappings of a Victorian first class railway carriage, which it rather resembled. My brother and I would ramble through the bulrushes in a small powered skiff which was equally stately, having an awning supported upon stalks almost as high as the boat was long. We met no-one, save a friendly lock-keeper who manufactured us some seats for the launch, out of what proved to be stop planks, those rather necessary items used for isolating a length of canal in the event of a burst.

Across the water stood a gaunt gateway, the last vestige of Tixall Hall, constructed in 1580; Mary, Queen of Scots, was, inevitably, a visitor (an involuntary one, I learn, as she was held a prisoner).

The visit by John, Martin and myself was, of necessity, terse. The old Wide atmosphere still prevailed, even if the houseboat had gone and the reeds had receded farther. We executed a great looping turn, stared northwards at the gateway, southwards at the woods of Cannock Chase, then turned back westward in order to rejoin the Trent and Mersey.

At Armitage there is a full blooded tunnel, 130 yards long and hewn through the solid rock, which hereabouts is red and more like papier-mache imitations at the local drama club than the real thing. It was possibly the first-ever tunnel to be built with a tow-path and was for many years unlined, although recent fissures have compelled the installation of steel braces. Armitage was always a bat stronghold and, as *Swan* thumped through in the late evening, these denizens of the darkness staged their customary mass exodus. Although there had been no regular commercial traffic along this route for some fifteen years, sufficient pleasure boats passed that way to keep the bats well exercised.

Armitage Tunnel, 130 yards long and cut from the red rock

We moored for some pre-bed sustenance at another pub, which, like so many, had started to acknowledge canals once again by providing a means of access from the waterside. The increasing presence of cursing holidaymakers from the water, thrashing about in the vegetable gardens and hammering at back doors, has not gone unnoticed by the breweries, many of which have installed delicate little mooring stages. We monopolized a whole row of bollards, before moving on to a leafier and less patronized part of the canalside. Here, none too early, we went to bed, a difficult undertaking in my case, as I had mislaid the torch. Quite apart from some abrupt confrontations between head and chain, I found it difficult to discern my bedding in the inky gloom. Climbing into a twisted sleeping bag and, at last falling back with a gladsome sigh, upon a movie camera tripod, as I did, is not the best of send-offs for a good night's rest.

Too soon, I was jolted awake again; a motor narrow boat, a maintenance craft from nearby Fradley, had contrived to smite us a shrewd blow in passing. It was time; through our engine room bulkhead I could hear the time-honoured ritual of starting the Gardner. First the blowlamp was ignited, to the accompaniment of several clicking pumps, a short hiss and another highly vocal search for matches. At last the lamp reached a dull roar as it attained maximum heat output and was brought to bear on the cylinder head. At this juncture, John and Martin always conducted an intense academic discussion on such

Above left: The Swan Inn at Fradley. Right: *A Brindley bridge at Great Haywood, junction of the Trent and Mersey and Staffordshire and Worcester canals. The Wide lies about a mile beyond the arch*

matters as the nuances of governor design. Then followed several rapid clicks of the injector, a short silence while a loop of rope was fitted to the flywheel stud, then a single abortive *punk* as the engine failed to fire. More discussion, more clicks; the engine usually started at the second attempt and at this point I would get up.

Fradley Junction is one of those spots where, for me, it always rains. I regard it as something of a frontier post, for here the attractive countryside comes to an end and a flattish cheerless stretch begins, reaching a nadir at Burton-on-Trent, but improving again beyond.

It rained for most of the day, a day in which many hours were spent in contact with the bottom of the canal. Few narrow boats used that stretch and, frankly, I was not surprised. *Swan* was running aground under every bridge, bumping her way over we knew not what. A friend of mine, Bev Portman, who the previous winter had worked an experimental load of timber down the Trent and Mersey had described how he and his wife were frequently compelled to offload the cargo onto the towpath. Although not so encumbered ourselves, we found conditions exactly as he outlined them: appallingly shallow.

Near Derby the locks become 14 feet wide and if that city had devoted greater effort to preserving the Derby Canal it could now be something of an inland port. Instead the waterway is abandoned and was almost unnoticeable as we passed in the dusk.

The day's end found us approaching Shardlow, bowling along before a very strong wind which would sweep *Swan* broadside as she waited for each lock to be filled. The late afternoon had brought a crop of converted narrow boats, winding through the reeds towards us, piloted by figures in motor-cycle togs or the flowing plastic robes of the latter-day Noah.

We blasted into Shardlow in the dark, our headlight sweeping over a pleasure boat which was moored too near the entrance to the lock. We managed to avoid being swept on to her by the wind and kept *Swan* pinned in forward gear against the top gate. As lock operation in the dark was becoming a fraught and anxious operation we decided to halt at this juncture, before someone tripped over one of the many obstacles present or, worse still, skipped blithely into the lock.

Shardlow was built as a canal town and still has many of the original buildings from when Brindley constructed this eastern terminal of his Grand Trunk Canal. Nowadays Dobsons Limited are building cruisers on the bend through Shardlow and the place still has an active character which makes it most attractive.

Beyond lay the Trent, which, after the cramped passage through the bulrushes of the Trent and Mersey felt like the Ganges. We passed through one river lock, under one embryo motorway, waved furiously at some gaping construction workers and sallied down to Trent Junction, a cross-roads of the waterways, where we intended to turn off and up the River Soar.

Left: *Marker at Shardlow. Preston Brook is the northernmost point of the T and M.* Above: *Old warehouse at Shardlow. Boats at one time loaded and emptied within the archway*

Chapter 11

The Valley of the Soar

Were it not for a rash of notice boards, the River Soar might slip unnoticed into the mighty Trent. It joins its big brother surreptitiously, in a weir stream, and voyagers like ourselves, fresh from the Trent and Mersey Canal, could easily ignore it, probably with disastrous consequences.

The Erewash Canal, a withered arm of the Grand Union empire, adds an element of complexity by running in from the north. Horse-drawn craft wishing to travel from this and into the Soar had to traverse the Trent, at times a raging torrent. A rope-operated ferry used to exist for this purpose but has long since disappeared. Years ago, too, a pair of narrow boats were carried away down the Trent, over the weir at Thrumpton, and the crews were drowned.

Aboard the *Swan,* all was serene. In a deep water channel, the boat moved much faster, behaving a little less like a plunger in a pump than on the narrow canals. Martin and I reached into the recesses of our scientific minds and calculated that with her 70 foot hull, *Swan* could theoretically move at the square root of (2 x 70) mph, i.e. over 11 knots. We were not, of course, doing anything like this speed, but it was nonetheless a relief to accelerate above the grinding snail's pace which had been forced upon us by the over-shallow, under-maintained Trent and Mersey Canal. John steered and also polished up the brasswork which any self-respecting narrow boat eventually acquires. I sat forward, writing a letter, watching the fields and woods slip by and wondering how long such an idyllic existence could continue before one of our intermittent crises developed.

'Actually we're a bit short of water at the moment', the lock keeper told us at Red Hill, the first lock up the Soar. Mindful of the rain which had filled my boots the day before, I had anticipated a first-class inundation. My previous voyage in this region had been downstream, the only direction possible at the time, in a river so swollen that a few blades of grass were the only indication of the fields alongside. It had been an exhilarating if dicey passage, our hired cruiser skimming under bridges with millimetres to spare. The culminating incident on that occasion had been an abrupt encounter with some closed flood gates across the channel, and a meeting of even greater violence, with the bridge alongside, which had prevented us from being swept over a weir. My brother Peter happened to be shaving at the time and had a narrow escape. We were all spared any

Above left: *The Trent, near the junction with the Soar.* Right: *Archetypal canal pub. The* Fishermans Rest *stands on the northern shore of the Trent beside the first lock on the Erewash*

further excitement for the next two days, however, for during that period all boats were barred from moving.

The Soar forms part of the Leicester Section of the Grand Union. Its existence saved the builders several million tons of earthwork although they were still compelled to install a number of locks, all of them fourteen feet wide and technically capable of taking a barge, as distinct from a seven foot narrow boat.

At Loughborough there is a lengthy section of artificial canal, much longer than the average lock cut. It embodies a short branch, turning off at a T-junction. Approaching from the south, John failed to see the signpost and steered *Swan* straight ahead and up the dead end. Slowly and painfully we were obliged to back out again, using the long shaft to keep *Swan* on the straight and narrow.

Beyond, and in the country again, the river was as delightful as ever. It is not unlike the Upper Thames, with the added pleasure for the voyager of being able to work the locks himself. We spent the night at Thurmaston, just north of Leicester and were directed to a good mooring by a man who approached us at the lockside and enquired about the *Swan*. It turned out that he had once been among the crew of a steam-powered narrow boat, owned by Fellows, Morton and Clayton, the great canal carriers. This company continued to operate steamers until the late 1920s, finally abandoning them because of the large crew required and because of the valuable cargo which such bulky engines displaced.

Fellows, Morton and Clayton soldiered on, and even after nationalization, boats were to be seen in their livery. Finally, the last red cabin side was painted over in British Waterways

The Soar a few miles above its confluence with the Trent

blue. At the same time, traffic to Leicester dwindled and for many years the Soar bore little commerce of any kind. Nevertheless, Fellows, Morton is still a revered title here, as in the remotest corner of the canal system. The title 'Josher', now synonymous with a certain type of fine-lined narrow boat, stems from the nickname for all Fellows, Morton craft and comes in turn from Mr Fellow's christian name, Joshua.

On such a note of heavy nostalgia we repaired to the town. On the way, I was startled by a violent sneeze in the grass beside the path. Whipping round with the torch, I confronted an extremely confused and abashed hedgehog, obviously full of remorse for the panic he had engendered.

The next day we entered Leicester and met an old friend. A small group of working boats were assembled above a lock. The boatman obligingly hopped over to open the bottom gate for us and as we drew near we saw it was Jack Monk. 'On the Leicester run now', he told us, and outlined his trips down the Trent to Nottingham and Newark and along the Witham to Boston. He was working for the firm of Seymour-Roseblade, which in its regrettably brief life as a carrying company was attempting to develop timber haulage to

Leicester and to re-establish waterborne trade in that area. Why such traffic ever left has always baffled me. The British Waterways Board, although proud that Leeds, for instance, was flourishing as an inland port, was quite complacently writing off points further inland, presumably because handling facilities there would have had to be created and because the waterways there needed many further improvements. At Leeds on the other hand such conditions already existed when the Board took over. What maddens me is the persistent refusal to look beyond the status quo. Leicester could be an inland port, so could Derby. The Midlands could be crossed by a wide waterway. Many outsiders have suggested this, time and again. The insiders, those in control, have never raised such a voice.

Jack Monk told us that his son, aged sixteen, had taken command of his own motor narrow boat, doing short haul work for Leicester Corporation. He also showed us a further vessel, which was of his own making, for in addition to being a skilful engineer, Jack was also an excellent model maker. His latest product was an electrically-propelled motor narrow boat,

Left: *Soar lock, a standard Grand Union structure of barge width.*
Above: *Jack Monk with model motor boat at Abbey Park, Leicester*

about four feet long called after his own craft, *Neptune*. The hull had been fabricated from a solid chunk of timber, hauled from the canal.

Farther on beyond Jack's mooring, the waterway runs through the centre of Leicester itself, at one stage through a wide cutting which, despite its grandeur, attracts few visitors. Our thumping passage up this waterway boulevard was observed by a solitary policeman who gazed at us through the railings, and looked in two minds about tackling us for trespass. In the city, stretches of artificial canal alternate with lengths of river; *Swan*, emerging from part of the former into a particularly tortuous example of the latter, failed to negotiate a bend and hooked her prow under the low bridge above one of the many weirs. With some difficulty we disentangled her and blessed the absence of any strong current. In times of flood these bends must be tricky to say the least. We all wondered how many boats in times past had been wedged broadside across the faces of these weirs and how many boatmen had, as L. T. C. Rolt describes, saved themselves by clinging to the underfaces of the bridges as their boats were swept beneath.

A few miles beyond we left the Soar for the last time and plodded on up to Foxton. Although the countryside was beautiful once again, it was largely obscured by heavy rain of great penetrating power. Dusk found us in the middle of the last flight of locks, being goaded along by a British Waterways engineer who wished to padlock the top lock as soon as we had cleared it. He and I would simultaneously drop our bicycles in the grass and, from opposite sides of each chamber, gaze morosely back through the rain, waiting for *Swan's* headlight and the quickening pulse of the engine to signify her departure from the previous lock. Working up these flights had been a slow process, as practically all gate paddles had been allowed to fall into disrepair and had often been removed altogether. Each lock took an age to fill, and from time to time the gear was of a non-standard size. This would add an extra straw to the lock wheeler's burden. Soaked and grumbling he would have to return down the towpath for a smaller windlass and cycle forward yet again through long wet grass and a path which was scarcely discernible in the murky light.

The engineer told us that, by using a diver, they had been able to cut down delays caused by faulty machinery. Only that very day a paddle had split and had been stopped up in a matter of hours.

We pressed on for Foxton, into the sweeping bends and bramble bushes which characterize this waterway. As it was now completely dark I had to stand in the bow with the torch in order to guide John round the bends. Occasionally the helmsman would miscalculate and I had to make a rapid choice between being plunged with some force into the midst of an overhanging thicket, or of retreating ignominiously from the flailing branches.

Above left: *Weir at Leicester, beside Lock No. 41*
Above: *Monumental paddle gear, Lock No.41*
Left: *Leicester again; weed in one of the river sections*

Finally, long after midnight, *Swan* panted into Foxton, her crew nursing various wounds incurred by contact with the hedgerows. Ahead lay the staircase of ten locks with, a further twenty-odd miles beyond, the Grand Union Main Line. This we intended to rejoin, just ten days after leaving it.

Chapter 12

Foxton and Beyond

At Foxton stands a very steep hill, with one canal at the bottom and another at the top. By means of ten staircase locks, these two are connected.

Swan lay in the pool below the lowest lock, ready, once her crew had mustered, for the assault. Bright sunlight had replaced the rainclouds of the day before and had tempted out a group of locals who were leaning over the parapet of the bridge above us. Gazing straight into my abode in the hold, they discussed, with some fervour, the lateness of our clamorous arrival the night before, and also the nature of our business. Since from my sleeping bag I could see them, it gradually dawned upon me that I was under discussion also. A mobile person is, for some reason, better equipped against conversational barbs than a recumbent one; accordingly I arose.

Staircase locks are not separated by short stretches of water. The top gate of one lock is also the bottom gate of the next. Thus, once interned, a narrow boat needs no steering whatsoever. If left in forward gear when ascending it will even push open the relevant gates on its own, provided, of course, that the crew have let in the appropriate quantities of water. Unfortunately a boat going up a staircase cannot pass another coming down and so, at Foxton, the builders divided the works into two staircases of five locks each, with a short pool in between.

Alongside is the site of the celebrated Foxton Inclined Plane, a comparatively recent innovation, which was, alas, dismantled again shortly after its opening in 1900. Two great tanks would trundle sideways up and down a ramp on the hillside, the one counterbalancing the other. Ideally each caisson would contain two narrow boats, but traffic was sporadic even then. Keeping the winding engine in steam proved too expensive and in addition the contrivance was beset by mechanical troubles, usually the collapse of the steel rails upon which the tanks ran. For these reasons the Foxton lift was abandoned after a year or two.

We wanted to inspect the site of this phenomenon and accordingly thrashed about in the bramble bushes which had grown on the ramp. Little now remains, apart from the odd culvert and the foundations of the engine house. The linking arm at the top of the hill is now dry although it retains a few vintage patches of treacly swamp.

Foxton; the foot of the flight. The house in the distance marks the top

At the bottom of the plane, the other arm is still linked with the branch to Market Harborough. Entry is barred by a fence and a Private Property notice. Viewed from beyond the barrier this area looks positively Amazonian in its luxuriant vegetation and would make an angler's paradise.

The locks remain intact. These, with the flight of seven at the other end of the summit level, form the only barrier between the Thames and the Trent for boats over 7 feet in beam. Their replacement would surely be the first priority in any modernization scheme for the waterways in general - together with a basic programme of dredging.

A short pound midway up the Foxton staircase just enables narrow boats to pass. The water has been drained off for repair work and a ground paddle culvert is just visible to the right of the further lock

The Foxton Inclined Plane. Though constructed in 1900, little trace remains of it today. Dismantlement took place in the 1920s, when all steelwork was removed

Boats entered the lift at this pool. The ramp up which the caissons travelled extends away from the right, but is now completely overgrown and barely recognizable

Husbands Bosworth Tunnel, on the long winding pound at the summit of the Leicester Section

A partial collapse in *Swan's* administration had left us safely at the summit, but foodless and at the wrong end for the shops. On my accelerating descent by bicycle I just had time to notice some further holiday-makers closely engaged with side ponds, paddles and motor cruiser. My toiling return, laden with comestibles was as slow as my earlier journey had been precipitate and I had plenty of time to study them further and to digest the heat of the sun, the steepness of the incline and the attentions of a great snuffly hearthrug which, upon inspection, turned out to be a dog.

The summit level of the Leicester Section is both winding and enthralling. Few roads come near it; there are no large towns. In a downpour it can seem the loneliest place on earth - not necessarily a criticism. In the middle of what proved to be one of the hottest days of the year, it provided a striking illustration of rural England, almost free of despoiling features. Leaving John and Martin to bumble slowly through the woods and cornfields, I rode ahead to the village of Husbands Bosworth. The towpath was so little used and in places the hedge so thick that riding proved difficult. There were no anglers, and correspondingly no litter. Dragonflies flicked above the water as I slowly pushed on beneath the blazing sun.

On returning I took over the tiller and settled down to the contemplative business of negotiating the winding twenty-odd miles to the next lock. Because the deep water channel is so narrow, *Swan* is compelled to travel slowly in such stretches. If, on cutting a corner,

The motorway crosses the Leicester Section at Watford Gap

she touches bottom she tends to become unmanageable. She will plug over to the opposite bank in a most determined fashion, taking her bewildered helmsman with her and jarring him to the back teeth if she rams, say, a concrete abutment. This happened to me.

Because progress was so slow, and there were no locks on which to exert ourselves, Martin, still on some kind of keep-fit jag, set off with John on some minor route marches. I could see their heads occasionally above parapets and hedgerows but their course by road was always more direct than *Swan's* and inevitably at each bridge two smirking faces would be waiting.

We moored at Crick where, in addition to the wharf, there is a tunnel, haunted of course. The following morning we discovered an insufficiency of paraffin to start the engine blowlamp. In my search for a source of this cheap but none the less precious fluid I found myself wobbling on to a roundabout beneath the M1 motorway. Sports cars and breakdown wagons were whirling into the roadway at a fantastic speed. A cranky cyclist clutching, as best he may, a milk bottle, handlebars and an empty paraffin can, is out of place in such an environment and was lucky in this case to escape without serious damage.

Although the motorway is some two miles away from Crick Wharf, a dull rumble of noise drifts across the fields. At a later stage in the journey I scaled a fence to the service area in the hope of buying some film and found a startling contrast with our canal life. We wondered how many motorists at Watford Gap service station knew that the Grand Union Canal (Leicester Section) skirted its perimeter. Few boatmen, unless they are stone deaf, can ignore the motorway.

Canal ghosts seem thoroughly mixed up. I am fairly sure now that the names Kit Crew (Harecastle Tunnel) and Kit Crewbucket (Crick Tunnel) have all been garbled out of Kidsgrove Boggart relating to Kidsgrove near Harecastle. Boggart is a northern word for spook and all the other names must have been hideously confused by some chronicler, perhaps writing down the incoherent utterances of some toothless veteran of the waterways. Crick, Kit, Bucket, Boggart, Crew and Grove have all suffered through the years.

Pondering on this dialectical nightmare, I stood on the bow as John rushed *Swan* into Crick Tunnel. I was shining a torch idly at the walls and waterline and was suddenly disturbed to see a snake, about two feet long and swimming hard. As the tunnel is almost a mile long and as the snake was roughly at the middle, I assumed that it was either an excellent swimmer or that it lived in there. Perhaps I can start a new canal ghost story and in twenty years' time will be reading of Snake Crickhandle or some such and wondering, with avid curiosity, how the legend all began.

Fellows, Morton & Clayton boats Bison *and* Dawley *en route from London to Manchester in 1926. The towline leads through blocks right back to the butty steerer, allowing its length to be more easily adjusted*

The motorway negotiated by canal underpass, we reached the excellently maintained staircase at Watford (Northants) and rejoined the Grand Union Main Line. This really ended our explorations, for now we were back on a waterway we had already covered. Uxbridge, our starting point, was now a mere two days' journey away.

It was a voyage which exemplified the several changes which have recently overtaken the waterways. Although commercial traffic had declined catastrophically, there still remained sufficient to enliven the helmsman's day. There are few more heart-stopping sights than a low heavy bow materializing through a blind bridge hole, towards which, with equal inexorability, a pleasure boat is heading. My vividest-ever memory of such a circumstance is of, years ago, treading on a bar of soap aboard a boat called the *James Brindley*, at the critical instant of reaching for the gear lever. A gargantuan boatwoman with a mop fended us even further into an overhanging thicket and told us some undeniable truths.

If commerce has decreased on the Grand Union, the number of pleasure boats (which also represent a form of commerce) has risen in direct proportion. Standards of performance

Above left: *Author, blowlamping.* Right: *The derelict arm from Buckingham, looking towards the Grand Union Main Line*

vary wildly. Several times we discovered a crew waiting eagerly, if vainly, for a lock to fill, blithely unaware of the water which was cascading out again through open paddles at the other end. Water is a precious and expensive commodity which, in times of stress, may have to be pumped back to the summit pound. A Grand Union lock requires, I believe 56,000 gallons to fill; each time a boat passes through, say, Braunston summit level, it removes 112,000 gallons, which is a lot to have to find again, particularly if a summit level is short. In times past the water from the Watford-Foxton level used to be sacrificed into the Main Line in order to keep the London-Birmingham traffic running during heavy droughts.

Reservoirs exist in quantity, although their function is unsung and often unknown, even to the people who use them for fishing or dinghy sailing. On the Grand Union Main Line alone there are thirteen reservoirs. On the Crinan Canal, in Scotland, is the shortest summit level I have ever seen, a mere three-quarters of a mile, and here a substantial pool has been created amongst the crags and boulders, in order to prevent even the most sporadic traffic from draining the canal dry.

The Crinan is spiritually a long way from Wolverton where, just north of a short spasm of urban bleakness, stands Rennie's aqueduct across the Great Ouse. This superseded an earlier structure on the site, which was erected by a sub-contractor; it was a botched job and duly collapsed, with Heaven knows what consequences, for there is a twelve mile pound here. According to Robert Aickman, the bases of the original piers may still be seen

Rennie's Aqueduct across the Great Ouse, near Cosgrove

in the river below, although I have yet to see them myself, despite several searching attempts. Nearby, the derelict Buckingham Arm runs wretchedly to the west, just upstream of Cosgrove Lock.

Thus we retraced our furrow of a fortnight earlier, spending an evening at Marsworth, then traversing the Chilterns in the traditional heatwave. *Swan* shared a few locks with a narrow boat conversion, through the open windows of which I observed crockery and a complete range of ladles, spoons and other kitchen impedimenta descending like hail as the boat rocketed forward into a gate. From this our fellow-voyagers deduced deficiencies in their reversing system and, perhaps mercifully, released us to travel onward on our own. Expresses pounded past on the adjacent railway as I busied myself upon a swing bridge, or attempted both to steer and to eat lunch (which is easy enough in long pounds, but tricky to perform with aplomb at the locks). We joined another converted narrow boat, the *Stirling Castle* of Harecastle fame, and, being both well equipped in crew and in staunchness of craft, made reasonable time from then on. Gongoozlers materialized in brigades at Cassiobury and stood in the way of several smuts which, also, by tradition in this stretch, were beginning to find their way from the chimney.

Stirling Castle left us at Harefield, turning off for a mooring in one of the gravel pits which appear to grow larger at every inspection and which are giving the Colne Valley the aspect of an inland sea. Denham Deep, a whackingly cavernous and stygian lock, was reached and passed. Urban Uxbridge loomed and at the last lock of all we pulled one gate open

Above left: *Swing bridge at Winkwell on the southern side of the Chilterns.* Right: Swan *follows* Stirling Castle *through the bends at Cassiobury*

with a rope attached to the boat, as normal boatman's practice dictates when descending a hill. The technique is to take a line round the handrail on the gate and there attach it with half a rolling hitch. In tension, the knot tightens and with engine in reverse the gate should open. Thus a single-handed boatman, or anyone who wants to save effort, can climb back aboard as the water starts to fall, later using the engine power to open the gate.

The knot should undo itself as the boat roars past; on this, the last lock of all, it didn't. Thus we approached Uxbridge with John steering, Martin going through the motions of packing up and myself feverishly splicing, in order to provide us with enough rope to moor by. We came alongside, pulled into our space, had a wash and shut off the engine. Although it seemed an age since we had left the same spot a fortnight before, the time had not in any way dragged. It was just that so much had happened.

Chapter 13

Underground Movement

A general yen for more exercise drove John and myself to revisit Dudley the following spring, together with some girl friends. Since our earlier and abortive visit, the tunnel had returned to its former function as a thoroughfare, under the auspices of the impressively entitled Dudley Canal Tunnel Preservation Society. Diesel engines and exhaust fumes being as inseparable as they are and ventilation in the tunnel being bad, the place had become a stronghold of the leggers, a fraternity long believed to be extinct.

As there was no towpath and as no horse could be persuaded to lie on its back and walk along the tunnel roof, human feet were compelled to do the job. At 3,127 yards the tunnel is the longest in regular use (the longest of all, the 5,415 yard cavern at Standedge in the Pennines is inaccessible by boat). To leg a boat through such a distance calls for a unique and demanding posture, as well as stamina of the highest order. We decided to try it.

Inland waterways are often difficult to detect from the road; therein, of course, lies their saving grace. The fanatic, like myself, must develop a keen eye for the inconspicuous parapet by the roadside with perhaps an unnaturally horizontal hedge beyond. The environs of the Preservation Society headquarters are at Tipton, the canal itself passing beneath a dual carriageway complex of impressive acreage. A thin straggly, and possibly rather shabby, line of water may catch the corner of one motorist's eye in a hundred. Once you're upon that water though, the automobile is inevitably forgotten.

Dudley Tunnel is one of the oldest in the country. It was opened in 1792, but for years before, limestone had been mined in the area. These old mines, a great labyrinth, are in several places connected with the tunnel, and this is really part of the fascination of Dudley. Some of the bore is lined while, in other sections, the inside widens into great caverns. On our own journey we encountered a posse of small boys who had somehow got in via the interconnecting galleries under Dudley Zoo and were roaming about a large fissure extending up and away from the canal-side. They had torches, while our own hard core of canal fiends-cum-potholders were armed with acetylene lamps stuck on General Patton style helmets.

In 1962 the tunnel was officially closed, 'thrown to the wolves' as Robert Aickman said at the time. The Preservation Society was formed to stop the wolves getting too strong a hold of it, although the structure remained beneath the possessive thumb of British Waterways.

Attempts have been made to develop a fume absorber for the engine exhaust; until the happy day of its perfection, however, a hard core of youthful, and by now fighting fit, members are compelled to slog through by foot. The boat used is almost invariably one of the old motor-less Birmingham day boats or joey boats. Call them what you will, they are amongst the most basic type of narrow boat, with the great advantage that tourists can be packed aboard like asparagus tips in a can. The men forming the propulsion unit are situated on the poop, sorry, cabin, at the after end. They lie on this and leg. Sometimes, however, the roof drops too low. Then the leggers may have a welcome rest; as momentum carries the boat long, they can contemplatively examine the brickwork as it skims a millimetre or so above their respective noses.

Having blazed through Birmingham's tangled streets, we tumbled without ceremony into a waiting joey boat. Richard Jones and Dave Apps, two of the youthful luminaries of the Society, introduced themselves and engineered us a privileged position at the stern. Meanwhile a trudging line of slaves towed us relentlessly towards the tiny portal under Dudley Hill.

Beyond the first entrance there are two intermediate cuttings, open to the sky, before the tunnel proper begins. One of these openings is Castle Mill Basin, within the grounds of Dudley Zoo. Here the canal runs into a triangular pool beneath steep cliffs. Running off out of the basin is the Wren's Nest Tunnel, leading to limestone workings which were opened in the mid-nineteenth century.

Castle Mill can be an eerie place. Richard Jones told us how a small group of members had been bringing the boat back late one evening when a man and boy appeared in the entrance of the abandoned Wren's Nest Tunnel. The two stared at the passing boat and walked across the water before disappearing. A year or so before, a man and his son had been drowned in the pool.

We pushed on into the tunnel, the big acetylene lamp on the bow lighting the way ahead. Fortunately Dudley is a dry tunnel with few drips of water from above. It holds some pretty hellish memories nonetheless. In the mines branching off the main tunnel the limestone was dynamited by men working up to eighteen hours at a stretch. The stone was loaded into small boats and ferried out to the surface. Later some of the lads took us into one of the adjoining shafts and showed us the gunwale of one of the small double-ended boats, just visible through the fallen shale.

Left: Castle Mills, where the tunnel briefly opens out into a basin. A preservation Society tour is in progress. Above: A party of geologists at the Tipton end, 1917

The first of our party to try legging, and the only girl to do so from the entire boatload, was Lin. We passed on through galleries of rock and undulating brickwork and through The Jail, a lined section in which any boat over the precise 7 foot beam is prone to stick. The number of craft suffering this horrific fate is not recorded. One wonders also if any boats happened to be passing when the southern end of the tunnel collapsed into the unlicensed workings of a free-lance miner who had cut directly beneath the canal. This happened in 1884 and explains the much neater brick lining and portico at the southern end.

The labyrinth at last negotiated, the assembled multitude took its lunch; we genned up on the local folklore and partook of pork scratchings, a disturbing local delicacy available in sixpenny bags. It resembles early coinage and is just about as digestible.

Having bounced our teeth about in this fashion we set off to inspect the Park Head locks, rendered impassable at the time of closure by such devices as the (official) sawing off of balance beams. If restored they would give access through the Stourbridge Canal to the River Severn. Considering its proximity to industrial Birmingham this area is surprisingly attractive, although the local council had not helped by permitting a revolting tip to spew about the area and even into the canal itself.

Near at hand is Netherton, a remarkably large tunnel by British canal standards. It was built to relieve the intense traffic which, by the 1850s, was clogging Dudley with boats (and leggers). As a through route the Dudley Tunnel gradually became redundant and its main interest is now a historical one. The Preservation Society took over the running of this canal, with the full approval of British Waterways and some day hope to throw it open to other boats, presumably towing them through with the fumeless craft now under development. In the meantime there is a lot of work to be done and a lot of money to be collected. At the time of our visit the most urgent demand was for £3,000 to pay for the strengthening of the railway bridge across the northern end at Tipton. This was apparently the only alternative to accepting the building of an embankment which would cover the northern end, though why British Rail should not be held responsible for the damage it proposes to inflict upon other people's interests escapes me.

It was this last proposal which caused the Society to be formed in 1963. Why bother? Perhaps the foreword to the Society's own booklet provides the best answer:

'Between the close of the eighteenth and the close of the nineteenth centuries, Great Britain passed from a rural to an industrial society, the first country ever to do this. In the Black Country many of the first engineering and technical innovations were pioneered. The relics of this early industrial age survive, but in rapidly decreasing numbers. It may soon be possible for children to see more visible evidence of the way of life of their medieval ancestors than of their great-grandparents.'

John and I legged the whole way back and lived to regret it. It can be very tiring work even with an empty boat, although it made us appreciate the luxury of *Swan's* redoubtable Gardner.

The northern portal. The short tunnel on the left was probably a loading bay for limestone

Chapter 14

Old Father

To the canal fiend the upper Thames promises the utmost in gentility. On the Thames there are 'sluices' in place of paddles, 'reaches' instead of pounds. The locks, far from being decrepit and nettle-strewn deathtraps, are lovingly tended by lock-keepers who actually do all the work - well, most of it anyway.

There are, of course, as in any tidy establishment, some rules which must be obeyed; more of this later. There was also, at the time, a fine distinction between a 'tug' and a 'launch', this amounting to the difference between eight pence and seven shillings and sixpence per lock, in the case of a boat like the *Swan*.

Notwithstanding some doubts on this score, John, Martin and myself resolved to voyage up the Thames the following year, and accordingly laid plans. These involved a desire on John's part to visit Henley Regatta, a rite for which he has much affection, having been bawled at by coaches and coxes alike over several years. We intended afterwards to push on into the canal system, then aim either for the Wash or for the Severn, this destination to be debated with greater fervour as we reached the crucial T-junction at the head of the Oxford Canal. We would also invite several friends to join us, for periods which, in the event, varied between a few minutes and an entire week.

Preparations were made. For months previously, the customary sawing, painting and cursing had made its impression on the neighbourhood of Cowley Lock. The Shovel, which stands beside the Grand Union Canal at this point, had been visited several times. So too had the Moreland Trading Company, a characterful dispenser of canvas and tarpaulins in St Pancras. The structures at the front, back and middle of the boat were then renovated to accommodate the various sexes.

We spent the final evening loading aboard the weird miscellany of objects which were to accompany us: a clarinet, two trumpets (with one mute), several books, in the naive belief that we might do some reading, a puncture outfit (for Lilos), the skipper's beloved brass polish and a mountain of assorted garments. We also annointed the hull sides with glossy black varnish, a fiendish fluid, the lowest by-product of the gasworks, which must be treated with the greatest respect. It contaminates adjacent paintwork, it spreads rapidly

Henley-bound; the lock-keeper checks the permit. Thames locks are well equipped, spacious and now largely electrified

from human hands to all sorts of astonishing places, it gives people asthma. However, it made the *Swan* look sleek and shiny so we put it on.

Long after nightfall I went back home to transmit some black varnish to the bathtaps and to write a couple of essential letters. The others would set off without me and I would join them at the foot of Hanwell Locks, just three miles short of Brentford and the junction with the Thames.

They were already waiting as I tramped up the towpath the next morning. The red cabin sides shone in the sunlight, the black varnish gleamed slyly and even Martin's cap had a freshly laundered look. *Swan's* single cylinder Gardner diesel was pop-popping as happily as when it was first installed; we set off, for Brentford, for Henley and beyond.

You can see this first stretch of canal, if you can spare it a glance, from the M4 motorway, as it slopes down at the end of the long flyover out of London. The directness of the road contrasts with the swinging bends of the Grand Union; at several such turns we met barges laden with timber. These craft, twice as wide as our own, work up the London River in the familiar trains but, once on the canal, are towed individually by tiny tractors. The men working them belong to some union or other and are barred from working the locks themselves. Hence the abundance of lock-keepers on the London canals.

The barge men and the narrow boat families have never as they say, got on. I gather this stems from the lack of consideration given to narrow boats which, unlike the tank-like barges, are floating homes, and thus all the more precious to the men, women and children

Boulters Lock, Maidenhead, forty-five years ago; hats were in fashion

Hambleden. The old mill above the weir survives almost intact

who operate them. This may explain, in part, why the working boat people have always preferred not to be addressed as 'bargees'.

We met two narrow boats at Brentford, the *Whitby* and *Moon*, loading grain for Wellingborough. In a fortnight's time we were to meet them again, in more active and unusual circumstances.

We also met some bargemen who seemed amiable enough, although with such large craft they could afford to be. The barges jostled like hippos round the electrified locks, below which they were being painfully marshalled behind a tug. After much procrastination, a gap was created for us to pass through in order to reach, at last, the very wide open spaces of the Thames.

From then on we had to develop new habits. Instead of attacking the lock machinery with as much ferocity as we could muster, we learned to wait patiently until beckoned forward by the lock-keeper. We had to get used to tying up, instead of banging around haplessly in the chamber, and we had, at all costs, to resist the Grand Union habit of stemming the gates. Otherwise the wrath of the Conservancy would be upon us.

In such a manner we reached Kingston for lunch (reaching shore, by dint of scaling a derelict coal shute) and Windsor by nightfall. Our hoped-for negotiation of a cheap toll had been thwarted at Teddington: 'Well, I've filled in a seven and sixpenny ticket for you now. A journey pass ? You'll have to get it at the next lock.'

At Molesey, the next lock, of course, they asked how much we'd paid at the previous one! Heads you win, tails we lose. The Thames is a pricey river.

Until Windsor is reached, the waterside is rather cluttered. There are too many houses and bungalows for my taste; far too many for the camper, as I have found on various canoeing expeditions. We passed Shepperton, where there is a new cut, the Desborough Channel. Built in the 1930s, it is far less interesting than the old loops of the river, which are well worth the detour. Beyond is Chertsey, of horse fame, and farther on still is Windsor. Here the river really comes to life at last and here a notice tells you where to go for a change of clothes, should you fall in (and survive). We spent the night opposite, beside the meadows. John, as owner, slept in solitary splendour in the boatman's cabin while Martin and myself took to the decked-in portion of the hold, still painfully limited in head-room, but furnished now with electric light and further mod. cons.

The following day, in even greater luxury, we had a meal ashore with friends, at Bourne End, wearing our carefully nurtured ties. I had to endure respectability for a further day, as we were due in Henley at the very apogee of the Regatta. A ticket to the Stewards Enclosure had been promised, an honour apparently not to be debased by entering in tramp's kit.

On schedule the *Swan,* with her crew now swollen to well over a dozen, passed through Marlow, through Temple, Hurley and Hambleden Locks, to the long straight reach below Henley. There the assembled multitude paused in mid-lunch to watch one very long, narrow and, I hope, gay, boatload chug sedately towards the town quay.

Chapter 15

A Look at the K and A

It is tempting to compare Henley with Cowes. Both have an annual fiesta, attended by a hard core of devotees, who display what is, to the outsider, an awe-inspiring fanaticism. At Henley, so many people are talking about rowing, or wearing puce blazers, or bellowing technical encouragement, that I begin to wonder how such a dreadful gap in my own education has gone unplugged.

In several respects, however, Henley differs from the Solent scene. As someone perpetually bewildered by yacht racing, a participant sport if ever there was one, I find it refreshing to see immediately who has won each event. In rowing, there are no handicaps, formulae, yardsticks or computerizations to be gone through before the victors emerge from the ruck. On the other hand it is possible at Cowes to sail straight through a racing fleet, in fact it is sometimes unavoidable. Furthermore sails on the Solent make an enduring spectacle whereas rowing craft tend to flit across one's vision and disappear into the deep blue yonder.

At Henley the course is staked out and partitioned off. It resembles, rather, Epsom under flood, if that were possible, with the racegoers somehow oblivious of the fact. *Swan* slid along behind the pickets, her speed curtailed by the adjacent presence of so many glossy spectator craft. Martin was interned below, making himself look like a stockbroker in order to greet a girl-friend, the children in our party were (again) demanding up-to-the-minute information on the local fish; the author yearned for lunch. Rowing had been suspended and, all about, hampers were being unlatched and molars were champing, with due Henley refinement, into cucumber sandwiches and the like. Across the water the massed ranks in the Steward's Enclosure were wading into their Pimms while, in the pub just beyond the bridge, an Irish team, early casualties in the competition, were well and truly launched on yet another day's festivity.

We made fast at the public moorings which Henley Council so thoughtfully provides. Our now numerous crew dispersed into foraging parties and, in due good time, I found myself in the much vaunted Steward's Enclosure. At half hourly intervals, two determined teams would flash by, one usually in front of the other. For the rest of the time, there was quite sufficient spectacle in the watchers themselves. It was here that I observed what must have

The Regatta. Two years after purchase, Swan *arrives in Henley Reach*

been the most elaborate floral hat of all time, worn by a young lady of admirably compatible appearance. Regrettably, I had left my camera on the boat and was therefore unable to record this vision. Henley can indeed be attractive.

Whisking through a sample of the myriad guide books on the Thames, I find that the stretch between Henley and Reading is generally rated second only to the Cliveden Reach, at Maidenhead, in the scenic league tables. It is certainly attractive enough, although my own favourites are the lonelier, less disciplined reaches nearer Lechlade. As I have decided to eschew scenic descriptions of the Thames, I include this paragraph to reassure readers that the river is, by and large, still beautiful.

Later in the evening we were joined by Margaret, a friend of mine, and by Albert Barber, another old confrère, cartoonist, book designer and nowadays inmate of the BBC. As all the previous guests had departed there were now just five of us left to disport ourselves

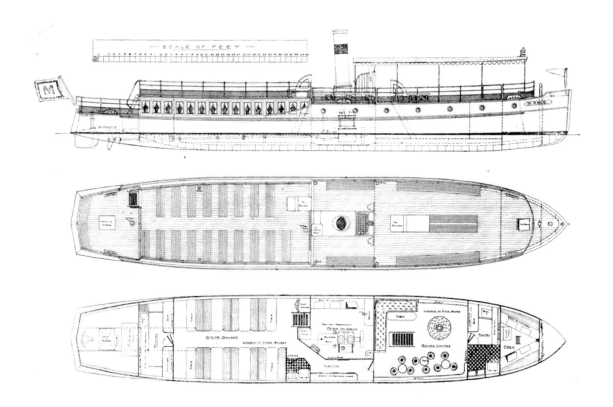

Early motor passenger boat, intended for work between Richmond and Oxford. Capacity was 300 passengers and the engine a 70 h.p. Kromhout

upon the swings, slides and roundabouts of the public park. In this fashion, we worked ourselves into the state of near exhaustion that on the *Swan* traditionally accompanies the end of the day.

The reach above Marsh Lock, tree-lined and sparkly, is one of the most sumptuous on the river. It was into such splendour that we departed, leaving the hubbub of the regatta astern. Inevitably, before very long, an incident had occurred. Our temporary decking across the hold was swept up by a projecting fender at the entrance to a lock. Martin and I surveyed our stateroom, now reminiscent of a collapsed mine shaft. Several baulks of timber, of the proportions of railway sleepers, had bounced upon our beds. We drew some obvious consolations and stopped at a sanitary station in order to render our sleeping accommodation, and our Elsan, suitable for further use.

Sanitary stations are fascinating installations, usually located on islands, so that only those privileged enough to travel by boat may inspect them. Years ago I accidentally camped on an abandoned sanitary station but was forced to depart in mid-meal by a collapsing tent (the pegs just would not stay in the ground) and by a gradually dawning aura of fever and fermentation. Enthralling though these stations are, with their tanks, their taps and their handles which you must turn three times, I cannot deny that it is pleasant to have a boat to return to.

Above Henley is Shiplake, where Tennyson was married, and Sonning, where the lock garden was awarded the Thames Conservancy prize for twenty-five years in succession, two typical examples of the sort of stuff which can be culled from the gazetteer. One item that is often overlooked, although less frequently nowadays than formerly, is the Kennet and Avon Navigation, which adjoins at Reading.

The Kennet and Avon is a shadow of its former self. To inspect it, it is necessary to be in good walking fettle, although the traditional canoe race still takes place between Devizes and Westminster, despite certain absences of water and the presence of an hysterical swan which, as the citations would say, presses home its attacks with the utmost disregard for personal safety.

The Bristol Avon most people will have heard about. The Kennet I once worked on for a few days, in the tripping boat *Enterprise*. We used to carry parties as far as Burghfield, about four miles above Reading. This, because of an unworkable lock, was as far as we could get. I liked the Women's Institute parties best; once the canopy over the boat, which was supported on a gaspipe framing, buckled spectacularly when we caught it on a lock gate. Several Institute members had narrow escapes and declared the trip a tremendous success. Once too, I whipped up a gate paddle far too speedily and drenched a vicarage party in the bows.

One of Salter's 'steamers' (now motorized), long a standard sight on the river, glides into a lock chamber. Man in the hat is Albert Barber

The Kennet at Reading, shortly before demolition work began on the terraced houses

Bruce Tunnel, Savernake. This is the eastern portal, the inscription plaque is just visible above the arch

There was also a swing bridge, from which the authorities, in their wisdom, had removed the balance weight. Manipulation here involved daring leaps into space and a nicety of timing that would not have disgraced a circus trapezist.

There are some staggeringly beautiful stretches on the Kennet and Avon and some notable historical relics. There are pumps, aqueducts and a splendid soaring flight of twenty-nine locks at Devizes. At Savernake in Wiltshire, diesel-hauled expresses thunder through the local station. When I went there that summer, shortly after *Swan's* trip, there was a 'quicker by rail' poster in one of the windows, despite the fact that the station itself was closed (it's now been bulldozed into oblivion). After blundering about in the undergrowth and inadvertently trespassing on railway property, I discovered the canal tunnel which passes directly beneath the station.

Over the eastern portal is a plaque commemorating the opening of the canal, at a time, incidentally, when the administration of the Thames was in a state of shambles. Indeed it was the sad condition of the upper Thames which forced so many of the southern canals to ruin. Nowadays the Thames above Teddington is very efficiently administered by, I believe, forty-one conservators. Previously there had been 10,000 commissioners, who had managed to achieve very little. Charles Hadfield, in one of his very comprehensive histories (*British Canals*, David and Charles, Newton Abbot) says 'By the time the Thames Conservancy was set up ... and an efficient administration was established, the Thames and Severn, the Wilts and Berks, the Basingstoke and the Wey and Arun tributary canals were moribund, the Kennet and Avon had passed into railway ownership, and the Londonwards traffic from the Midlands once brought into the river by the Oxford Canal had long ago been diverted to the Grand Junction.'

However, back to the plaque at Savernake. It says:

'The Kennet and Avon Canal Company inscribe this TUNNEL with the Name BRUCE In Testimony of their GRATITUDE for the uniform and effectual Support of The Right Honourable THOMAS BRUCE EARL of AYLESBURY and CHARLES LORD BRUCE his Son through the whole Progress of this great National Work by which a direct communications by Water was opened between the Cities of LONDON and BRISTOL ANNO DOMINI 1810.'

The canal link between the two rivers took sixteen years to construct, and cost £1 million at that time. It eventually passed into the clutches of the dreaded Great Western Railway. The more recent history of official gerrymandering on the Kennet and Avon will be familiar to many, certainly to those who have felt it worth contributing to the Kennet and Avon

Left: The 29 lock flight at Devizes. Right: A Devizes lock, with paddle gear still standing

Canal Trust and work for restoration. John Gould of Newbury fought against illegal obstruction for many years, his own craft having been sealed into the canal by a suddenly declared 'stoppage'. After much pestering an official statement was extracted from the then Docks and Inland Waterways Executive. It said, 'The work is to be undertaken but it will not be possible to complete it before the middle of next year' - that was in 1950! Later a parliamentary deputation was to point out that this obstructive policy was in breach of at least ten statutes and that the Transport Commission was probably liable to an automatic penalty of at least £5 an hour.

Needless to say the canal is still only open in isolated stretches though the Trust is doing its best with working parties and is now experiencing great co-operation from the waterways authorities. After the writs, lawsuits and the brazen neglect of this waterway, we are now in the position where, we hope, the damage can be righted, though the pace to date has been painfully slow, and the Ministry of Transport has escaped scot free of any onus for the damage it has caused.

The Kennet and Avon apart, Reading is not a particularly enlivening riverside town, having erected its gasworks in the most prominent position available. We staged our own little adventure, just beyond, however, as the *Swan* slugged her way upstream. Faint strangulated cries from the helm indicated that A. Barber, Esq. was in trouble. He had been abandoned to steer a lonely furrow while the remainder of the party disported itself upon the deck. Now it seemed that the chimney had decided to unburden itself of two years accumulation of soot; most of the hotter globules were landing on Albert, who strove valiantly to maintain his course under this Pompeii bombardment. Glowing soots the size of sugar lumps were to be discovered in his hair and, later, on his clothes. After the engine had been stopped, and the chimney allowed to clear, we staged a post mortem on Albert's shirt; this, after due discussion, was adjudged to have been one of his best.

We set to work on the mess, for engine soot can be oily, and restarted the faithful Gardner. The helmsman was retrieved from the bank, to which he had retired to nurse his wounds and take some photographs, and off we set, travelling once again hopefully, if slowly, in the direction of Oxford.

Chapter 16

Upstream to Oxford

A nod and a wave are the most you generally get from the passing traveller on the river. In rarer instances he may shout at some misdemeanour or, as happened to me on one exotic occasion, he might even throw tin cans. Otherwise, from the point of view of sociological study, life in the wide Thames reaches is fairly dull.

On the canal, things are much matier, for here a pioneering spirit still pervades the system. You often have to squeeze your boat within a fraction of someone else's and there is a fair chance of a collision, or of going on the mud, or of falling in, or any combination of all three. The occupants of passing boats can be the subject of withering scrutiny under these circumstances, although it is advisable not to discuss them immediately, as sound travels excellently across water. I have frequently heard confidential observations being bellowed by people who believe their engines to be noisy enough to drown anything.

It is at the Thames locks that the different boatloads confront each other with a jolt, for the lock chambers are big enough to be shared. At the height of summer, mixed fleets eye one another shrewdly and jab themselves apart with boathooks. Slops of tea are absent-mindedly poured through portholes onto the occupants of skiffs and fathers try desperately to discipline their families without becoming the censure of all eyes.

This gritty counterpoint was well illustrated as John twirled the big gear control wheel and eased *Swan* forward between the lower pair of gates. An assorted armada was waiting to follow us in, just as soon as the lock keeper signalled, when a shiny luxury cruiser pushed her way past the patient queue of lesser fry and charged into the lock.

'We can't fit in with this coal barge here!', sang a voice from the bow, inviting an obvious rejoinder from neo-collier Sheldon on the *Swan*.

'I hope you're not going to damage my nice black paint with your great white boat.'

At Whitchurch Lock, higher up, the other occupants were far more courteous. We had a pleasant chat with the assistant lock keeper, a student on vacation, who was sporting a striped boater. I have always had a nostalgic affection for this piece of the Thames, ever since camping on an island just below Goring, in the nearest approximation to the idylls

Left: *The more elegant aspect of the river; punting in the middle reaches.* Right: *Clifton Hampden, where the bridge looks deceptively ancient. It dates back only to 1863*

conjured up in the *Boys Own Paper*. It has always seemed a civilized and yet attractive spot, and it seemed so now.

The further up the Thames you go, the more Jeromey it becomes and a pleasant time can be had by all. Martin had devised a towing bridle for his air-bed, a dangerous innovation in the view of Margaret and myself, who foresaw a sudden rending, to be followed by a hiss, and perhaps a gurgling cough. As Martin's scientific training has been thorough enough to forestall such a catastrophe, his demise was not forthcoming. He skittered merrily along in tow behind the *Swan*, a picture of health and vitality and one of the few people ever to voyage up the Thames on his bed. We pulled him back aboard before anyone could ask if he had a licence.

We spent the night at Shillingford. Albert insisted it was Ambridge and hopped about the field where we were moored, in an attempt to take the definitive photograph. A vast platoon of cows had somehow tramped from the horizon without appearing to do so, and were now examining us at close range in the way cows do. Albert's attempt to encircle them failed dismally, as his animated foreground refused to co-operate. An extended rodeo developed in which the photographer became increasingly at odds with his subjects and was eventually compelled to give up.

We retired to Shillingford Bridge, where there is a floodlit hotel. It was very pleasant to sit outside, provided one didn't mind arc lights and the clouds of nocturnal insects that are attracted by them. An expensive drink is not really improved by the addition of sundry midges, all with a death wish. Too soon, the crew of the *Swan* retreated back across the picturesque bridge. Thence, by devious routes which at one stage included someone's back garden, we reached our field, and the boat. Here the day's exertions took their toll and we conducted a semi-somnolent eating session.

We still had seven locks in twenty miles before we were due to leave the Thames at Oxford. This meant seven more lock-keepers. On the whole the keepers are a good tempered crowd who have to witness endless near-disasters and, very occasionally, the real thing. Although the recent mechanization work has tended to separate them from their flocks, no method has yet been devised for the remote-controlled inspection of the lock passes, permits, licences and other paper paraphernalia so beloved of the Conservancy. A telephoto lens suggests itself, so that the man needn't leave his cabin. That day has not yet arrived, thank goodness, so the lock-keeper is still a force to be met and very occasionally reckoned with.

We had our first and only real engagement with a keeper shortly after setting out from Shillingford. In fact we Had Our Name Taken. This in itself constitutes a form of disgrace, so I'm told. The bone of contention was *Swan's* Gardner engine which we wouldn't stop when ordered to do so. One of the Thames byelaws stipulates that engines must be turned off if more than one boat is in a lock. The previous twenty-six keepers had not thought fit to draw our attention to this detail, nor did any of the ones remaining. Engines should be stopped on the grounds of safety and inconvenience to other users. Anyone who has wrestled with *Swan's* hot bulb diesel will know that these qualities are best attained by keeping the thing running. To restart, a highly tempestuous blow lamp would have to be brandished for about ten minutes or so. The engine might then have started in reverse, as it sometimes did, or have staged some of its other idiosyncrasies. It ran very well once it was running; we found it best to keep it that way.

The lock-keeper told us to get something more convenient. The convenience of the widely fitted petrol engine is debatable, in view of the fires, explosions, and deaths which occur every year. I know that the Thames Conservancy is very conscious of the safety angle, having attended one of the fire-fighting practices it regularly stages for its staff, but in my experience, petrol engines are at their most dangerous when being restarted. Shortly after *Swan's* voyage I was about to start the auxiliary on the sailing boat I share; petrol was dripping out of a jammed carburettor-onto the starter motor terminals. It would be interesting to know how many of the Thames burn-ups occur for similar reasons. At Abingdon we did indeed discover the charred hulk of a respectably sized resin-glass cruiser, one of two black spots in an otherwise charming scene. The other was an ugly outcrop of modern housing, not ugly because it was modern, but because of the crassness of its siting.

At Abingdon the remnants of the old Wilts and Berks Canal can just be detected on the outside of the big bend. It doesn't do to stare at it for too long, for there seem to be an unusual number of hazards in this area, from pleasure steamers, which are manageable, to swimmers, who can be hair-raising in their disregard for a swinging boat propeller.

Albert had departed back at Clifton Hampden, one of several delightful villages, with an apparently aged arched bridge which is, in fact, a bare one-hundred years old. Albert and I both pelted along the towpath on photographic business, murmuring old saws about exposure and in grave danger of each taking a picture of the other taking a picture. We then split up, Albert to hitch-hike to London to spectate at someone's wedding, myself to rejoin *Swan* at the next lock and to admire the lockkeeper's sleek and self-possessed black cat.

In referring to Oxford, which we reached by mid-afternoon, I must join all the other authors who have heaped derision on its lack of water-consciousness. One can only conclude that the University accent is on the literary arts rather than the visual, for there are several boring boathouses and a most distressing region near Osney Lock. The more satisfactory

College barges, moored below Folly Bridge, Oxford

Above: *Stuck on the weir near Folly Bridge.*
Right: *Entering the Oxford Canal*

boathouses, which were erected later, and the few remaining college barges heighten the grisliness of some of the other props. Quite incredibly, Oxford has turned its back on the river.

Osney Bridge is the one all the dire warnings are about, regarding headroom, or lack of it. We discovered, nay lit upon, a more significant hazard just above Folly Bridge. Totally unmarked and unheralded, the remains of an old weir lurk beneath the surface. *Swan*, drawing well under the statutory 3 feet 3 inches, ran hard onto it. According to the men who very obligingly came over from the adjacent boat station, this sort of thing happens all the time. A crowd gathered on the bridge as our engine clattered more and more urgently astern. *Swan* was very firmly on indeed, just under the engine room. Our approach, desultory at first, became more and more businesslike and after about an hour we were free. The most efficient method, we had discovered, was to get into the water, insert one of our robust top planks under the boat and literally lever her off. In lieu of any warning notice, I commend this approach to other ensnared travellers.

There are two entrances to the Oxford Canal. One is through the Duke's Cut, so called after the Duke of Marlborough who owned and, as far as I know, still owns this brambly link. The other approach, the one we chose, took us deeper into the heart of Oxford, to join the canal through a single narrow lock. This lock, touchingly tiny in comparison with the Thames jobs, basks under the glory of two alternative names, Isis Lock and Louse Lock.

The latter is the more accurate, for this really is dead dog country, spurned by the Oxonians. There used to be a terminal basin on the Oxford Canal, suggesting all sorts of exciting possibilities. It has in fact been filled in, and Nuffield College now stands upon it.

A railway swing bridge also bars the passage to the canal. This connects the main line with a small marshalling yard and it used to be a major sport to insist on the right of passage. Squads of railwaymen would grudgingly appear to coerce this bridge into moving. The lock-keeper at Whitchurch had been most insistent that we take this path ourselves. When we got there we found the bridge already swung open, as nowadays it is, at weekends. Boats entering and leaving the Oxford Canal are no longer a novelty and it is now obviously less trouble to close the bridge for the occasional train than to open it for the passing pleasure boat: a sign of the times, perhaps?

Chapter 17

Shallows and Lift Bridges

Full of the exhilarations of being on our own again, we opened up the 'speed wheel', jammed *Swan's* jet control lever into the on-load position and zoomed forward out of Louse Lock, Oxford. There would be no more lock-keepers to hold us back, no more sessions of idling at the behest of a white-capped figure, while nothing happened at all. We were our own masters now, ready for anything, set for a record-breaking run into the Midlands.

The Oxford Canal greeted us soggily as *Swan* thumped into the mud. Within seconds we had been reminded of the basic tenet of the narrow canals: that the bottom is too near the top. After an hour's dragging progress, during which something like two miles had been covered, we were resigned to it.

Martin came out to peer across some playing fields at his old school. I wondered if any of the boys I saw brawling beyond the cricket roller would ever go cruising themselves in later years. If they do I hope the canal will be nearer its statutory depth of 3½ feet instead of the 2 feet or so to which it has declined.

Although the Oxford itself may not amount to much, the Oxford Canal is a lovely one, and almost entirely rural, with the exception of a melancholic stretch at Banbury. We tied up at Thrupp, a charming little village and, following some brief by-play with the mooring spikes, repaired to the pub, where Margaret roundly defeated us all at bar billiards.

At the time of the Stratford bonanza, one of the sprightliest of the pilgrims had been an elderly boatman named Joe Skinner, a well-known and much feted figure on the waterways. He and his wife Rose had stayed independent of any large company until the day of their retirement. They had been the last of the boat people to do so, the last of the 'Number Ones'. The Oxford Canal had been their stamping ground and they knew Thrupp well. The *Friendship*, which they took to Stratford, had remained their home; I can recall meeting them years ago on the Oxford, with the boat loaded with coal. Their mule Dolly struggled along a withered towpath, while Mrs Skinner sat in the stern wearing a large bonnet. It had been a disturbingly nostalgic occasion.

Perhaps because of the lesser efficiency of working pairs of boats through single width locks, the larger companies tended to eschew the canal down to Oxford. It had

Above left: *Thrupp*. Right: *Joe Skinner, Oxford Canal boatman and the last 'Number One', or owner/boatman, on the narrow canals*

correspondingly become one of the last redoubts of the Number Ones, who tended to own single horse-drawn craft. In several of the canal society magazines there have been some splendidly evocative accounts by Ike Argent, whose father had been a Number One. Stories of shooting the antiquated navigation weirs on the Thames and of carrying a boatload of horseshoes from the Kennet are matched by the hard times of a hard winter on the Oxford, when the father had to take his horse out on rag and bone collection in order to support his family. As interest in canalia continues to grow, I can only hope that these stories can be made available to a wider public, as they deserve to be.

At the pub in Thrupp, we saw some examples of canal paintwork which belonged to Joe Skinner's father but, for all their long standing they look as if they were hung there yesterday. While in the pub I also heard an intriguing conversation, regarding the apocryphal Thrupp Duck Derby. This esteemed event was in fact a straightforward duck race, staged annually down the canal at this point, the contestants being egged on by a line of worms suspended by strings from the bridge. Can anyone throw some more light, or at least some authentication of this intriguing legend? I heard about it just before closing time.

Just beyond our mooring point was a right-angle bend, plus an assortment of moored craft which made it essential that the said bend be properly negotiated. To add extra complexity;

there is also a lift bridge, one of the pivoted drawbridge constructions which are characteristic of the southern Oxford and which stem from the financial stress the waterway underwent during its building. Generations of inland navigators have faced the prospect of being snuffed out like gnats beneath a steam hammer as they have stealthily crept under these poised but finely balanced structures.

Swing and lift bridges can be a source of limitless entertainment; Derek Gittings, manager of the Dudley Tunnel, once told me how he watched a canal pundit studiously wind a large cast iron counterweight down on top of his head. Bridges of the Thrupp type are less risky to the operator. All he has to do is to walk up one of the inclined balance beams until the bridge topples; to shut it again he just walks back and up the inclined roadway. It is advisable to give at the knees on each occasion. Unfortunately the operator has to be retrieved afterwards, for towpaths nowadays are better adapted to steeplechasers than to people who wish to get on at the next bridge (assuming that it is of a non-lifting type). A certain amount of judicious engine work is involved, during which a boat like *Swan* is exposed to the vagaries of the wind and to the demoniacal anti-clockwise twist, which often occurs when you put her astern. This accomplished, all the bridgeman need do is to close his eyes and jump.

Thus we left Thrupp, and shortly entered the mile-long section in which the River Cherwell runs through the navigation. The entry lock into the river is diamond-shaped, although it still has the single 7 foot wide gates which are customary to the Oxford Canal. The Diamond Lock regularly features at that erratic and sometimes tormenting institution, the Boat Club Lantern Show. I have heard some pretty wild guesses at the reason for this unusually shaped chamber. I think the correct answer is that this is a very shallow lock with a very slight fall; it is enlarged to allow as much water to be drained into the canal as is taken out when a boat uses the next lock farther down.

There are many similarly attractive spots. Shipton on Cherwell is one, although here a council estate has insidiously encroached. At Upper Heyford I once fell off the bow of a boat as it was entering a lock and just about beat the all-comers record for clambering out onto the towpath. That incident apart, the place has very pleasant associations, as have Somerton (a very deep lock here), Aynho, and Kings Sutton.

By dusk the long-suffering *Swan* was grumbling her way into Banbury, lurching over the debris in the channel in a manner that made me fear for her bottom. 'Come boating on the waterways and get stuck': not a very inspiring motto, but an apt one on all too many narrow canals. In circumstances such as these the reduction in the British Waterways deficit means very little. I cannot for the life of me see how it will cost less to maintain a canal for pleasure rather than commercial purposes. Obviously money can be saved by allowing the water to get shallower, but eventually the decline will have to be arrested. Maintenance will then be comparable with the costs of deeper waterway and a lot of British Waterways' customers will have been scared off in the meantime.

Our speed had now reduced to well under 1 mph and we were all beginning to get rather angry. Suddenly everything happened at once. A hired cruiser whisked round the bend beyond a bridge and, sensing our presence, swerved decisively into a thicket which only marginally cushioned its impact with the abutment. While her outboard shrieked our own Gardner engine stopped dead as some extra resilient obstacle embraced the prop. It takes a lot to stop the *Swan's* flywheel; I wouldn't like to try it, but a motor tyre, for such the object proved to be, can do it with ease. By the time we got the thing off it was completely dark and the hire cruiser incident had faded into the mists of time; we had all got wet and I had cut myself. It was quite obvious where the tyre had come from, for a few of its

John and Margaret at the Diamond Lock into the Cherwell. The lozenge-shaped planform of the chamber is just visible in the background

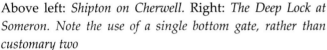
Above left: *Shipton on Cherwell*. Right: *The Deep Lock at Someron. Note the use of a single bottom gate, rather than customary two*

stablemates, plus sundry redundant pieces of motor car, were to be observed teetering on the brink nearby.

We got the tyre off by restarting the engine, then tentatively letting in the clutch. Eventually a lucky pull from the boathook flipped the propeller free and we proceeded into the Stygian gloom of night-time Banbury. We passed through the next lock, negotiated the spiked gate which has been so charmingly erected across the towpath at this point, and moored at Tooley's yard for the night. A motion that the tyre be wrapped up and sent to Banbury Town Hall was passed unanimously and promptly forgotten about.

L. T. C. Rolt's classic book *Narrow Boat* (Eyre and Spottiswoode, London, 1954) has a lot to say about Banbury. This is a deservedly popular volume, superbly written, if occasionally irritating (to me) at times. It has a poetic and timeless quality which far, far exceeds anything I can attain; it should be required reading for all those with power to influence our environment .. Narrow Boat is an account of a canal voyage undertaken in 1939, with Banbury the starting point. I do not know if Mr Rolt has visited the town recently, but I have a pretty shrewd idea of what he would make of it. The waterside area has been devastated and is now a prize example of the cheerless jarring chaos which the *Architectural Review* so admirably pinpointed in its celebrated 'Outrage' issue. We ought to do better than this.

Ironically, after filling in a basin in order to create the bus station, and shortly after our own visit, Banbury formulated plans for 'a marina ... to cater for the growing popularity of pleasure cruising.'

Mr Herbert Tooley was still there, running the same boatyard from which the Rolts' *Cressey* started out. The narrow boat *Dragonfly* was in the dry dock for the final stages of her conversion to a pleasure boat for Major Grundy, David Hutchings' successor as manager of the Lower Stratford Canal. Other boats were moored about, waiting their turn, and it was a pleasant consolation to know that, Banbury notwithstanding, the Tooley tradition still endured.

Our departure the following morning was delayed while we shopped for a bicycle, an implement we deemed vital in the efficient working of locks. John's earlier machine having advanced way beyond decrepitude, we needed a replacement and acquired a gleaming specimen for £8. Thus equipped, we set sail for Cropredy, one of the prettiest villages and a welcome contrast to our stopping point of the night before.

Just as Alphonse Picou's clarinet solo in High Society has become the test piece for aspirant jazzmen, so the summit level of the Oxford Canal is the real examination ground for narrow boat steerers. In terms of general tortuousness, the two are very similar. Between Claydon and Napton, we had to voyage 11 miles in order to travel between two spots which are only 4½ miles apart. We all had a go, and twirled Swan round the corkscrew bends in grand style. Martin produced a weird black crispy garment as a gesture against the oncoming rain. Nominally a plastic raincoat, this distinctive, if desiccated, apparel had achieved the fibrous resilience of charred newspaper. I stuck to my donkey jacket, which

Below left: *Banbury where a bus station now stands on the site of the old basin. Chain link fencing and lamp standards add to the glamour.* Right: *Wharf on the Oxford Canal at Cropredy. The coal comes and goes by road*

does at least stay in one piece, even if it tends to blot up rainwater and retain it for several days.

This winding summit stretch is often cited as the best example of James Brindley's adherence to the contour principle and of his reluctance to build embankments and cuttings. In the light of Charles Hadfield's very thorough *Canals of the East Midlands* (published by David and Charles, Newton Abbot) it looks as if Samuel Simcock has to carry the can for this amazingly circuitous route. Brindley must nevertheless have approved the plans before his death in 1772, at which time Simcock succeeded him. Mr Hadfield talks of trouble with the local landowner, Earl Spencer, and hints at the necessity of avoiding locks or stopping places. This area has physically changed little in all that time; the most significant points on the route are Fenny Compton, Wormleighton and Marston Doles. Incidentally, two tunnels were built towards the southern end of the long pound, respectively 336 and 452 yards in length and separated by a 155-yard open section which was, strangely enough, of insufficient width to allow boats to pass. Protestations from the boatmen finally caused this tunnel to be opened out in 1870; at no point was it more than 40 feet below the surface. To this day the stretch is known as 'The Tunnel' to the working boatmen, although few have travelled through in the past four or five years.

At last the windmill on Napton Hill hove into sight. We descended the nine locks and, doing our best to disregard the downpour, moored up. Our big decision, whether to turn left or right at the top of the canal, had already been taken. Time did not allow us to try for the Wash, with its attendant possibilities of long delays due to the weather, the vagaries of pilots or the protestations of the Board of Trade, which no doubt would be brandishing copies of its safety requirements. We resolved instead to turn up the Grand Union, then off it and via the North Stratford Canal to Worcester. We could aim for the Severn and, with luck, the Lower Avon, which joins at Tewkesbury.

Chapter 18

Through Birmingham's Countryside

Apart from some scrappy journeys in the Claydon area, our new bicycle had not really tasted blood. The Grand Union Canal provided us with our first real opportunity, possessing as it does some truly bicycle-worthy stretches on the descent down to Warwick. I leapt ashore, whirred the pedals vigorously and, with great aplomb, set forth on what proved to be a disastrous attempt to beat *Swan* to the next lock.

The hedges and grass were still fully charged with rainwater. I was wet within two minutes, drenched in four. Furthermore, the towpath in this vicinity did not really merit that title, consisting chiefly of dredged-out rubble, stacked willy-nilly behind crude concrete piles.

My injuries accumulated as I pounded through the overhanging hedgerows. With so many distractions, it was some time before I deduced that a puncture had occurred. Wet, saddle-sore and no longer caring, I bashed through the thicket to an adjacent road, and walked along that instead. 'Lock wheeling' from then on consisted of fiddling about with spoons in lieu of tyre-levers, in between moments of battle with the massive Grand Union lock equipment.

We had turned left at Napton, to take the same track towards Birmingham as *Swan* had followed the year before. Once again we flexed our windlass muscles and looked forward, with some apprehension, to the forty-six monumental locks, twenty-three up and twenty-three down, between us and the top of Hatton.

At the very commencement of all this hard work, we had overtaken Roger Polhill, who lived aboard a 16 foot glass-fibre cruiser and was taking it, single-handed, from Leicester to Bristol, 'in order to get more speed', as he said, indicating his forty horse outboard. An early encounter with some of the paddle gear on the Calcutt flight had been enough to convince him that it would be less exhausting to team up with us. By working through all these locks together, we were able to save him a lot of time at little extra cost to ourselves, once we had got a system going.

We met the horse-drawn hotel boat *Pamela*, hauled by Jim, the same big grey we had seen pulling the *Iona* at Norbury the year before. He was ploughing along in mighty fashion,

Locking down on the Grand union with Roger Polhill crouched on stern, Martin mending portion of dismembered bicycle

dragging the *Pamela* off the mud as if she had never been on it, and periodically shouldering his long-suffering attendant into the soaking brambles. Jim really relished work but, being so big and strong, was apparently expensive on towlines and also, presumably, on oats.

We sustained ourselves through Leamington with some beer, a pint each, purchased at The Two Boats and carried in our decorated water can. This experiment proved unsuccessful, for the vibration of the boat knocked our drink as flat as bilge water. If I say that its taste was in accord with my impression of the Leamington waterfront, I will probably confirm the suspicion that I hate all towns. I had better add, in haste, that Warwick is a comparative pleasure to pass through.

With various misgivings, *Swan* was eventually brought to the foot of the mighty flight at Hatton, as big, magnificent and stiff as can be imagined. It was late afternoon. First we met the British Waterways pair of narrow boats which carried cement along this stretch. They had just emerged from the bottom-most lock; a screeched conversation in passing yielded the vital information that the gates were being padlocked for the night. We all adopted aggressive stances, whilst I blew into one of our trumpets and, for once, produced an agreeably impressive result. As the locks were technically open until seven p.m. and as it was only five-thirty, we were on strong enough ground; the gate was unbolted again without further ado.

We would have to get to the top now, however jaded and decrepit we might feel, for mooring is forbidden in the short pounds which separate the locks. I assume this to be an official precaution against leaky gates, or half drawn paddles, which might drain the water from beneath a sleeping crew, perhaps damaging them in the process and inducing that dangerous state of mind which contemplates legal retaliation.

The crew were brought to action stations. Roger sat on *Swan's* counter and was held responsible for his own boat, which we were towing. He whipped it alongside ours as soon as we entered a lock and took whatever precautions he could against it being pulped between us and the opposite wall. I, as steerer, was able to help him in this respect. By keeping *Swan* in forward gear against the top gates, and with the tiller over, I could pin her against one wall. The water would surge in, violently at first, but gradually subsiding as the levels equalized. Martin, meanwhile, would run ahead and perform the necessary gymnastics at the next lock, which he would have ready for us to enter.

We approached each open gate at that finely judged rate which is all too near calamity. John would nip ashore as we entered and close the gate again behind us. Simultaneously, Martin would start to let the water in before galloping off to prepare yet another lock. Who said canals are leisurely?

There was one small scare, when I shot into a lock, only to find a small cruiser already in there, cowering behind the other, and unopened, gate. Her crew were going through the tedious and unnecessary motions of pulling both gates open before they emerged. We backed out and let them get on with it, which they eventually did. At least we now knew that the remaining locks would be in our favour, and it was in this belief that Martin had taken a few minutes off in order to drape the remaining skeins of his mummified macintosh over himself.

At the sight of this, the heavens opened and gave us all a good wash down before we moored at the top. Just to keep everyone in the party spirit, John announced that the battery had not been charging. A brief comedy was enacted, in which he and Martin analyzed the recalcitrant V-belt and, with a crisp rending sound, Martin caught a gesticulating sleeve in it. Then Roger half fell in, following which we all went for a drink, braving some thunderous lorry traffic in order to glean a few fragments of Roger's life story.

It turned out that he had been making a living repairing peoples TV sets, but now wanted a change of venue and hoped to join up with some friends at Bristol. He knew very little about canals and had been labouring under some terrifying misapprehensions about how far he had to go. He did have a bicycle, which was kept in his tiny boat. when he was outside it, and vice versa. He also told me about a programme of Himalayan folk music he had tape-recorded from the radio; this had inspired him to lead a party of fellow

Construction of the new locks at Knowle, during the modernization programme of the 1930s.
The old narrow locks are visible on the left

enthusiasts into the Quantock Hills where they could practice this newly discovered art in greater privacy.

A shy, yet engaging character, Roger had some unexpected facets. Unhappily he would be unable to accompany us on the next stage of the journey, for the locks on the Stratford Canal, and beyond, are of the narrow canal dimension, big enough for *Swan* only.

The Stratford Canal is entered at its central point, at Lapworth, via a mud-encompassed T-junction, which we made the customary botch of. First of all comes the contentious linking arm with its single lock, then another T-junction. On the left is the Lower Stratford, running down to Shakespeareville itself; I am happy to report that its water problems are now to some extent resolved by the laying of a pipeline directly across to the Grand Union.

On this occasion we drew a bead on Kings Norton instead, and turned right up the nineteen locks of the Lapworth flight. These have an irritating characteristic in that, however hard you try, the bottom gates swing open before you have time to let the water in. The slightest nuance of propeller control would set them off, and some heated repartee was generated. I subsequently discussed this point with a Willow Wren boatman, who had better be nameless. He said he let the water in first, before bothering to close the bottom gates. This robust, not to say slamming, approach is fairly typical of the working boat community. It is not to be recommended to amateurs.

I have canoed along the North Stratford in the dead of night, looking for one of the camp sites with which it is so singularly ill-endowed. In the end we opted for the towpath and prayed for an absence of horses. The waterway here is for much of its length in a cutting, and, although the everyday world is obviously close at hand, it is concealed behind the high scrubby banks. I always find the atmosphere here faintly menacing, possibly because of an encounter, years ago, with an elderly lady who was smoking a pipe.

Nearing Kings Norton we hit the shallows again. With great pomp and ceremony Martin and I had halted the traffic and raised a lift bridge, only to find that *Swan* couldn't reach it. She had gone aground when wriggling past, ironically enough, two boatloads of dredge. The cars piled up, whilst shafts were produced and the boat rocked free. After what seemed an eternity, John was able to ease the boat forward and across the bloodshot field of vision of the roadbound.

We collected several more items around the propeller, struck the bottom more and more frequently and finally ran the engine dry, having forgotten to pump the header tank full of fuel. The airlock bleeding committee was summarily convened and before the gaze of a solitary little girl, watching from the garden of a council house, we went about, our business. At long last the Gardner blew one of its inaugurating smoke clusters and we were on our way again; in due time we had passed Lifford Lane Bridge, scene of one of the earliest battles between canal preservationists and the forces of authority, and arrived at Kings Norton. Here there is a stop lock where, at one time, a marginal difference in level compelled the boatman to halt and be levied a toll on his cargo. The gates here are of the guillotine type and are much photographed and talked about. Judging by the gaps in the timbers, they obviously haven't functioned for years and boats can slide straight through the passage beneath them.

At Kings Norton we joined the Worcester and Birmingham Canal, a long-winded title which strikes terror into many hearts, by virtue of the vast number of locks on the descent to Worcester. For the first nine miles, however, there are none, and we bowled forward into countryside which was astonishingly attractive, considering its proximity to the centre of Birmingham itself.

Swan entered the northern portal of West Hill Tunnel, often spoken of as Wast Hill. It is dead straight, so that despite its great length - over a mile and half - it is just possible to discern the other end. If another boat has been through, however, the exhaust fumes cut down the vision and the far entrance cannot be seen.

There are a number of tunnels on the Worcester and Birmingham and by virtue of such fumes and by occasional distant sightings, it became apparent that we were overhauling another boat. This we eventually overtook on the Stratford Cut. John Gittings was steering, and obligingly waved us past. The last time I had met him, he was on the working boat *Yeoford*; this time his cargo was human, and included a band. The *Franklin*, converted, and with a full length cabin, none the less radiated bonhomie and visibly rocked as her contents surged to and fro under such an orchestral influence.

Left: *Moving up the Lapworth flight, nineteen locks in all.*
Above: *Guillotine gate at the Kings Norton stop lock. The gates themselves have not been in use here for many years and boats merely pass beneath*

The last tunnel before the locks is at Tardebigge itself and, although short, is impressive for having an unlined roof, blasted out of what I assume to be millstone grit. I remember watching a steam tug work through these tunnels with a loaded narrow boat in tow. I remember the horse also, which had been left to walk over the tops on its own and evidently knew the route by heart. That was in 1954 before commercial traffic ceased on the Worcester and Birmingham and before the terrifying local rule, that all traffic must keep to left, was revised. It is now, together with the Gloucester and Berkeley Canal, in line with the rest of the system and all traffic keeps right. It is typical of the canals, some would say of this country, that such exceptions persisted for so long. One wonders what dramas have been enacted in the tunnels as strangers tried to pass.

The name Tardebigge has a rural tinge and although this is an important spot on the waterways it is probably little known outside them. Like Bittall and Withybed Green, which lie even nearer Birmingham, it is a tonic to anyone jaded by urban surroundings. Here are fields, a picturesque wharf, a bend, a mysterious cutting and an elegant church spire up on the hill.

Here we stopped for the night, just beyond the smartly decorated narrow boat *Cactus*. After a sortie up the hill and a brief explosion of energy, when I buried the contents of the lavatory, we went to bed.

Chapter 19

Down the Slope

John was to be found the following morning, battering away at a squadron of flies that had invaded his cabin. He was employing a rolled-up copy of one of our heaviest newspapers arid posed as great a threat to the intruding crew as to the insect world.

Peeved queries of 'Using our *Sunday* – ?' were dealt with in mordant terms: 'Yes, it bores them to death!' The slaughter continued, with a break for tea. We huddled nervously beneath the steel tiller which, when not in use, hung poised between two straps directly above the bench seat. In weight and damage potential the tiller resembled a piece of scaffold pole, albeit decorated in the manner of Uxbridge Rock. It had already become detached at an earlier stage of the trip, half demolishing Albert and abruptly terminating his contribution to the mealtime conversation.

Breakfast consumed, we readied the engine for another day's toil. A horde of school children had arrived and were noisily embarking on the *Cactus*, moored a short way up the towpath. I excused myself from the washing-up on the ground of pictorial necessity and played a brief solo hand of 'hunt the camera' in our cramped and dimly-lit hold. Rushing in pursuit of the *Cactus* I found her already manoeuvring in the basin, with an empty butty in tow. I watched them turn off back towards Birmingham and for a few moments after they had disappeared into Tardebigge Tunnel heard soprano voices echoing from the vaults within.

We ourselves, facing in the opposite direction, were poised on the very brink of (a) the most heavily locked decline in the country and (b) a hard day's work. Tardebigge stands at the top of the Lickey Hills and, because Worcester is way beyond the bottom, *Swan* would have to lose altitude. There are fifty-eight locks on the Worcester and Birmingham, thirty-six of them in one flight. Doubtless, dozens of waterway fanatics will be gnashing their fists and girding their pens at this erroneous information, for there are really two flights, one of thirty the other of six locks only. In truth, I have never been able to tell where one lot stops and the next begins, so close together are they. I was once on a slave-ship which did the whole lot in well under two hours. In memory of that achievement, I subscribed wholeheartedly to the suggestion that we 'Take it easy this time'. Margaret, John and Martin were all equally in accord with this philosophy. *Swan* therefore entered

Tardebigge Top Lock on the brink of the Lickey Hills. From here 36 locks wind down towards Worcester

Cactus was the 100th motor boat built for Fellows, Morton & Clayton

and left Tardebigge Top Lock (the deepest narrow lock in the country, I believe) at a leisurely pace.

Across the fields is the Lickey Incline, up which gargantuan locomotives used to push one another with a sprinkling of wagons in between. When we were there, all the trains seemed to be dieselized and were making mincemeat of the extreme gradient. When the canal was first opened, the diesel engine, far less the diesel locomotive, was an unknown phenomenon, a life-span away into the future. Nonetheless, ingenious proposals were made in order to get boats up and down the hillside.

Alongside Tardebigge Top Lock is a pallid memorial to one of these attempts, some fragments of masonry and a hole in the ground. Here, for a few controversial years, stood a perpendicular lift, the prototype of a series of twelve which would take boats all the way down to Worcester. Its wooden caisson weighed 64 tons when filled and an equal weight of bricks was used as a counterbalance. Test runs were made and, according to Charles Hadfield, 110 boats were raised and lowered within twelve hours. Supplying the necessary winding power were two men; I'm very glad that I wasn't one of them.

William Jessop loomed on to the scene, as a consultant. His fair but gloomy prognostication - that the apparatus, was too complex - probably tipped the scales. The locks were built, the lift abandoned. Had the pro-lift faction won, I am sure the Worcester and Birmingham would now cease to exist. Delicate machinery would not have withstood the neglect and parsimony of recent years.

Halfway down the flight. The locks are easy, but with so many to operate it pays to have a bike

Martin having restored our bicycle, the locks proved easy to work, if numerous. It was a good opportunity for 'strapping', that is, using a stern rope in conjunction with a bollard placed for the purpose on each top gate. Thus, in Wild West fashion, the boat is stopped and the gate closed behind it. Meanwhile, the person who would otherwise be fidgeting uselessly at the top gate can be diligently applying himself to the bottom one, and letting the water out. So runs the theory. If performed with the proper nonchalance, strapping is a prestigious exercise in the eyes of casual bystanders. Otherwise, not so. I knew someone who rooted a bollard from the ground by over-diligent application of the rope, while, once, on the Leeds and Liverpool Canal, a boatload of coal burst its way through the bottom gates when the rope broke. On horse boats, of course, strapping is an absolutely essential technique to master, as there is no other way of stopping gently.

In addition to a reputation for salt, Droitwich was a prominent name on the dials of pre-war radios. The transmitting station there is still going as strongly as ever and Martin claims it is possible to pick up the Light Programme by way of the local wire fences. Droitwich

Left: Man meets machinery, Worcester and Birmingham style
Above: Strapping on the top gates, using a rope both to close the gate and (sometimes) stop the boat

also boasted an abandoned canal, of which more anon, while, just beyond, lay the site of one of Martin's Austin Seven incidents. These could be more accurately described as Narrow Escapes and the countryside is littered with their memories. Martin departed on a short pilgrimage to this particular locale and we picked him up later.

And so to Worcester. Events happened in this order, though not as rapidly: First we ran on to some object unknown (a double-decker bus perhaps?) which heeled the *Swan* so severely that I thought we must topple over. Then we ran on to a great reef beneath a bridge that was being reconstructed. Finally the canal became so generally shallow that *Swan* was performing more as a plough and could achieve nothing better than 2 mph for an entire pound. In this last stretch a small boy threw a selection of stones at us, with considerable deftness and accuracy.

The first incident, the toppling one, took place in the shadow of a faded British Waterways notice which still urged traders to 'Use the Waterways'. The paint was peeling.

The bridge incident we anticipated, as it is a fairly common one when rebuilding is in progress. There is always the likelihood of the old abutment or some such having toppled from the roadway. This does not happen on bridges over railways but is a commonplace on canals. Sure enough, we were aground. I backed *Swan* off and took her at a run towards the archway. An assembled populace watched from above and received a volley of exhaust gases. The back end of the boat rose some 6 inches from the water and grated horribly. Our momentum was, however, just sufficient and aided by some valiant pushing from the crew, sundry Irishisms from the construction workers, and much retaliatory abuse, we just made it.

The small boy we encountered standing beside a derelict Baptist chapel. Appropriately enough the remnants of an equally decrepit harmonium were projecting from the water. *Swan*, at this time, was moving across the landscape at roughly the speed of Big Ben's hour hand. We were therefore a sitting target for the various impedimenta this wretched little child felt compelled to throw. Helpless ourselves, it was an uplifting experience to watch justice materialize in the shape of a large policeman, who appeared in full regalia and into the arms of whom the child inadvertently rushed.

Elsewhere, on the water's edge, were other horrors. Mr Wigley (timber merchant), for instance, was sporting several cubic yards of tangled rusty wire which would very shortly be finding its way into the cut. If you ever go through Worcester and get such material on your prop, you'll know where it comes from.

I would rate the canal at Worcester about Force Nine in the Liley scale of impenetrability by boats. Force Six is what *Swan* barely floats in; Force Twelve is dry land.

King's Head Lock, named after a pub, and the last narrow lock on the canal, proved rather a tight fit. This only dawned upon us when we tried to get out. As the water goes down, and the steerer idly inspects the filthy oily walls which pertain in spots such as Worcester, he fails to notice that these walls are in fact tapering in. At least, I failed to notice. I put the boat in gear - she moved forward a foot or so, then stuck. The antidote was to back as far as possible into the lock, assign Margaret to rocking the boat, Martin to pull it (with all his might), John to let some water down through the top gate and myself to open the throttle. Provided all these activities coincided there seemed a fair prospect of emerging from the lock. We succeeded, and entered Diglis Basin. It was rather akin to finding ourselves transported from a farmyard puddle and out into the North Sea. We could actually alter course, without stopping dead.

Worcester boasts some more attractive facets. We ate in comfort and reasonably cheaply, Martin was able to find some replacement rainwear and Diglis Basin itself looked much improved from the tatty atmosphere I remembered.

The Severn, beyond, is one of my favourite rivers, one I have travelled all the way from Llanidloes, where it is little more than a mountain stream. The lower reaches have the flavour of a Mark Twain story, with tanker barges in place of the gilded stern-wheelers; somehow New Orleans seems just around the next bend. It is not possible to see too much beyond the shore, for the banks are high, if pleasant. A temperamental waterway, the Severn periodically floods, bringing with it much driftwood and dead livestock on such occasions. Big, wide and handsome, it is, however, a grand river at all times.

Disused basin at Worcester. Car dump in the background, neglect all around

The capricious Severn. Worcester in winter

Our entry to it was delayed in the barge locks at Diglis, our licence proving out of date. For the first time, we realized that the large figure printed all over this piece of paper related to the month of its expiry. No-one had told us, thus far. The matter was put right on some kind of promissory basis. British Waterways are much more human about this sort of thing than, for instance, the Thames Conservancy. Their lock-keepers and maintenance workers are, too, generally the most likeable of men, if frequently 'underemployed' and despondent at the post-war turn of events.

To say that we opened up the throttle on the Severn is not to say that we went speed crazy. I have to be very cautious here, as I know from previous experience that Severn devotees are very hot on this topic. Nonetheless, once through the big locks below Diglis (another licensing discussion here), we fairly bowled downstream. Past the big red cliffs, past Upton we sailed; past too, the entrance to the Warwickshire Avon, had it not been detected out of the corner of our communal eye.

Here was another junction and a choice. To the south lay the Gloucester and Berkeley Ship Canal, which doesn't go to Berkeley at all, but to Sharpness; its main function is to by-pass the least navigable bit of river, the stamping ground of the celebrated bore. I have voyaged

Deep water at last; out in the high-banked river, with a chance of moving to some purpose

Shapely hulk, now acting as bank protection on the Severn

through Sharpness myself; gazing soulfully down into the glutinous mud at the bottom of the ship lock and later, when the tide was right, venturing forth into the overfalls and currents of the Severn Estuary, a dubious sailing area for the uninitiated.

The Lower Avon, into which we turned at Tewkesbury, is far less salty and much more placid. It has some modest little excitements of its own, as we were to discover and, if not exactly storm-tossed, has a quirky history and has been the object of much recent endeavour.

Chapter 20

Cul-de-Sac

Although we didn't know it at the time, we entered the Avon with a cargo of bedsprings. These we had doubtless acquired in the sobering penetration of Worcester, and they were to cling doggedly to *Swan's* propeller shaft for some time to come. So far the only hint of their presence was the clouded and pained expression of the man at the helm, together with sundry grumblings from the area beneath his feet.

This apart, our entry into the Lower Avon was a happy one. Mr Brown the lock-keeper proved an excellent ambassador and, having created such a genial atmosphere, had no difficulty in winkling £2 out of us. This was the price of a seven-day ticket to Evesham, a return ticket, the Avon being a cul-de-sac. Like several other interstices of the waterway system, it is, incidentally, independently controlled.

The Tewkesbury lock-keeper now has a new house, built on stilts, not as a defence against alligators, but as a protection against winter torrents. The surrounding waterfront is pleasant, as befits such a town, and is also active, for barges bring grain to Healing's mill. Opposite the lock is a wall which, so we were told, 'most of the long boats hit', a neat and effective means of warning us not to do the same. We didn't - just.

Swan skirted various skiffs, negotiated King John's Bridge and with John (Sheldon) at the helm and a faint murmuring from the bedsprings, we pottered off through Twyning and round Bredon Hill. Margaret had left to return to work and there were only three of us now, John, Martin and myself. We toasted absent friends in warm pop and remarked on the blissful scenery.

A glance at the map will confirm that the Avon, as every schoolgirl knows, runs all the way to Stratford. At one time the upriver journey between Tewkesbury and Stratford was perfectly feasible. It was in fact frequently performed in the lengthy interval between the respective reigns of Charles I and the GWR. Following the intervention of Mr Boulton and the demise of the Upper Avon, the Lower portion, that stretch between Tewkesbury and Evesham, inevitably followed suit and atrophied shortly afterwards. In saying that the Lower Avon was reopened by a non-profit making trust, I am skimping a mass of detail, from the legal negotiations which made the Trust possible, to the pick-axe, saw and

Tewkesbury. The Avon flows almost surreptitiously towards the Severn, its weir stream passing under the iron bridge and behind the mills at the back of the town

frogman stuff of its members. The project was led, indefatigably, by Mr Charles Douglas Barwell. The work, to quote Robert Aickman, 'has been undertaken .... with fanatical enthusiasm, and in many cases, specially acquired craftsmanship; and it is no exaggeration to say that through the Trust a new and valued central interest has come into many lives.' Here are some sample statistics:

Purchase of Freehold Property and Navigation Rights, in 1951, cost £1,438, a low and yet oddly pedantic figure.

The derelict lock cottage at Strensham was acquired in 1952 for £419(!) More has been spent on this property since.

Work at Pershore Lock on the other hand totalled a mighty £12,484 and was completed in 1956.

The waterway became fully open in 1963, costs totalling £70,000.

With two exceptions, all the Lower Avon locks are do-it-yourselfers; they have their own idiosyncrasies. Nafford Lock, for instance, is tricky to get out of, being located hard on a bend of zero radius. Pershore, on the other hand, has a diamond-shaped lock chamber and is shallow at the sides. Those ashore run their own little gauntlets; several hazards here demand an eagle eye and a firm clutch on the National Health Card.

It was at Pershore that the last flash lock, or water gate, operated. Sluices would be raised and, after an eternity, the river levels would be near enough equal for the single gate to be cranked open. Then, by fair means or foul, voyagers could navigate the torrent, speedily if going downstream, slowly otherwise, if at all.

It was beside this gate that, as a child, I caught an eel, but failed to despatch it with the neatness that marks the expert. Quite understandably, the brute wouldn't stay still long enough to be killed. I won't go into any of the sordid details, but have since regarded eels with distrust.

We cruised through Pershore in the late evening, by meadows tenanted by heavyweight cattle and past the mill to which the grain barge *Pisgah* plies. Although the countryside was, if anything, more beautiful than ever, things took an eerie turn after nightfall.

We had moored in a narrow, fast-running stretch, with scarcely a house in sight. We ate, and succumbed to the inertia which always afflicted us as washing-up loomed nearer. Chins lolled forward on to chests, conversation lapsed into primeval grunts. In a last despairing effort, Martin and I consumed the remaining oxygen and headed for the door.

Outside, it was unexpectedly cold and misty. Leaves were whipping downstream on the fast-flowing surface of the river and, across the water, the willows and the bulrushes waved above the vapour. The scene was very reminiscent of the film version of *The Turn of the Screw*, and we hurried forward to the refuge of our bunks in the hold. The atmosphere was frightening; we both commented on it. Once in our sleeping bags, we felt even more scared, particularly when we heard the clump of someone coming aboard and felt the boat rock. Nothing further happened and we put it down to John, out on some nocturnal perambulation.

Next morning he addressed us quizzically.

'Did you hear someone come aboard last night?'
'We thought it was you.'
'I thought it was you.'

Everyone gulped and we moved *Swan* on. We never knew who the visitor was, if indeed we ever had one.

Above left: *Restoration work on the Upper Avon; construction of a new lock.* Right: *Eckington Bridge, near Bredon*

We reached Evesham, another pleasant waterside town where moorings are free and visitors welcomed. Here we extracted the bedsprings, which emerged, bronzed and fit from their experience, and we discussed the river with some other boat owners.

The Avon is so popular nowadays that it is difficult to visualize its earlier decrepitude; the quantity of cruisers roughly parallels that on the Upper Thames. Some day, perhaps, the section up to Stratford will be reopened and will link up with the Lower Stratford Canal, mentioned earlier. Such a connection would make all the difference to the canal, for circuit routes are always more attractive than dead ends. We had already met one hirer, at Worcester, who had assumed the Avon link was complete and who registered consternation at having to go back the way he had come.

David Hutchings, who did so much for the Lower Stratford Canal, is one of the men engaged on the Avon Problem. Work has now begun but, in general, the legal problems have been complicated. For instance, the river has changed its course since abandonment, and ownership and rights are open to doubt.

Above Evesham, therefore, we were in anarchic territory, beyond the protection of the Trust. It is possible to journey on for a short way, to a pub which is crammed to the gunwales with anglers and outside of which there is just room to turn a narrow boat round.

We had the misfortune to smite a dinghy in this topmost stretch. A tiny little boat sailed across our bows, apparently on starboard tack and with comfortable room to spare. We pressed on and, to our amazement and horror, the craft immediately went about and shot back on a reciprocal course, right under our bows. *Swan* doesn't stop as quickly as that, however determined the man at the controls (me in this case). For an awful moment I thought we would pulverize this strangely reckless mariner. However he emerged, bashed and angry, bumping his way down our hull. Neither side being in a mood of remorse; we had a crisp exchange as he passed. Perhaps fortunately, there was little time for an involved discussion of the matter. By the time we had managed to stop we were well beyond the point of impact. Our assailant had resumed his incessant broad reaching and had elected to ignore us. The matter was closed.

Throughout our voyage we had leaned heavily on *Gateway to the Avon* an admirable little booklet, produced by the Trust. Here we found the historical lowdown, and maps of all the biggest hazards. 'Shallows' are given great prominence, although these might well be classed as 'deeps' on other waterways!

On our return journey we were further aided and abetted by volunteer lock-keepers, who turn out on summer weekends. We found them, with all due respect, a mixed blessing.

Descending a diamond lock. The Avon lock chambers are remarkably short and narrow boats can sometimes only leave by opening the bottom gate on the side away from the boat and then poling the boat across

Mr Brown of Tewkesbury and Mr Jones of Strensham are professionals, well versed in locks. At other places we found ourselves at the mercy of less practised personnel and *Swan* suffered a bit in consequence. Being so long, she was in great danger of fouling the upstream cill, which many operators didn't know about. We would be pulled this way and that and as the locks are only just adequate in length, we had quite a time of it. However, the experience was rich in observation of the human condition and, as we found the Avon so generally friendly, it would have been churlish to berate a voluntary servant, however misguided his endeavours.

We avoided the worst types of damage and worked our way back downstream. It rained, and Martin and I took refuge in the hold, occasionally sloshing out into the downpour, in order to forestall further volunteers. At last we reached Tewkesbury, too late to pass through the lock and also, as it turned out, too late for a meal on the town. We moored in the weir stream, sallied up and down the wet streets and, discovering little grub of substance, retired to the cabin.

Chapter 21

The Severn, Stourport and the S and W

The Severn was in a good mood when we rejoined it, and had not elected to engulf us with the accumulated downpours of central Wales. We set off upstream in search of Stourport, a canal town; Martin gurgled happily into his clarinet as *Swan* swirled northwards. The Severn, as I remembered it, was remarkable for its sporadic convoys of tanker barges. These would descend like the Philistines upon the unwary, batting forward with cargoes of several hundred tons apiece and shovelling the river before them in impressive heaps. However, by the time we had reached Worcester, the point at which the most awe-inspiring of these vessels were wont to materialize, we had not met one.

Worcester itself is being built upon, rather nastily in places, but its riverside frontage still retains a certain grandeur. The *Radio Times*, in days of yore, would regularly usher in the cricket season with a photo of flannelled tourists deployed with the cathedral in the background. With almost equal frequency, the *Manchester Guardian* would feature Worcester racecourse, with the horses ousted by swans, as the river yet again excelled itself.

The locks on the Severn are monumental. They were erected in the middle of the last century to overcome various shallow stretches which had for a long time dogged traders. Oddly enough, vessels used to voyage as far as Welshpool before this improvement, but ceased to do so shortly afterwards. The last barges reached Shrewsbury at this time and, by the turn of the century, the navigable limit was the present one, a few miles above Stourport. The grooves of towlines are still to be seen in the arches at Bridgnorth and at Ironbridge.

Our reception varied wildly from lock to lock. The bush telegraph, transmitting the news of our out-of-date licence, was oddly inconsistent. One lock-keeper took our name, another charged us, I think, three and six. Yet another turned our licence over several times, stared at the huge figure four, signifying expiry the previous April, and said 'seems all right'.

Above Worcester the river gets even prettier. We were keeping a sharp lookout for the long-defunct Droitwich Barge Canal. We found it amongst the trees above Bevere Lock and *Swan* was tethered to a big elm while we explored.

The first lock in the canal is now embodied in someone's front garden, but I was able to yell across the fence and obtain permission to take a closer look. A great big doggie, of the St Bernard ilk, felt called upon to bound towards me as I entered. Fortunately it proved to be one of those animals which, when squared up to suddenly remembers some Very Important Business elsewhere.

We inspected the lock and its neighbour, which though shrouded in brambles, still retained half a gate, swinging in space upon a decayed hinge. The lock chambers proved in fair order and it was possible to stand on the upstream cill of one of them and examine at close quarters the massive curved slab, carved of stone, which lined it.

Through these locks sailing craft, the 'Wich Barges', used to journey to Droitwich for cargoes of salt. Doubtless they were bow-hauled along this tortuous waterway; hauling by men was once a commonplace on the Severn itself, although the towpath rights have since been allowed to lapse. Traffic up to Droitwich ceased during the first World War and abandonment followed at the beginning of the second. The water in the canal, incidentally, was saline.

The Wich Barges were versions of the Severn trow and were flat-bottomed but otherwise graceful sailing craft. In the winter of 1966, the *Butty*, journal of the Kennet and Avon Canal Trust reported the trow *Hannah* to be still afloat in Gloucester Docks, while the *Spry* was at Worcester. The corpses of others are to be found rotting at Lydney and other points on the Severn foreshore.

Above Bevere we met our first sample of current commercial traffic on the Severn, which, to date, had proved a strangely empty river. This consisted of a tug and two unladen barges. Whilst approaching Lincomb Lock, the last before Stourport, we saw another dumb barge being winched out. It was manned by a solitary old gentleman, who, having been whizzed from the lock chamber by means of some spirited work at the winch, was apparently left to his fate. He passed us, drifting aimlessly downstream, and pushing the big tiller without any noticeable effect.

On leaving Lincomb, we found a tanker barge and a tug waiting to enter. No-one seemed in very much of a hurry and we were in some doubt as to whether the tug would overtake the old man before he pottered over the next weir, four miles downstream, at Holt.

The Regent oil depot was located just beyond. We subsequently learned that the tanker we had passed was one of the last to come upriver, the traffic shortly afterwards being passed over to a conjunction of pipeline and heavy lorry. The pipelines I can stomach, in fact I am all in favour of the things, provided they are properly buried. That road transport

Leaving Worcester. Swan heads upstream, and north for Stourport

Entry lock to the old Droitwich Barge Canal. Fortunately the dog didn't bite

Commercial traffic is sporadic now on the river. This was one of the last tanker runs down from Stourport

is cheaper for the company I do not doubt; so long as we persist in the weird system of accountancy which itemises every penny on rail or water, but which fails to do anything of the kind on the roads, this situation will remain.

Soon we were off Stourport itself, wondering which locks to enter. There are two sets, one of barge size, the other consisting of four narrow locks. They all proved to be padlocked, it being early evening; the narrow locks, which we had selected, had apparently just been repaired. A small boy told us his father had done the job, being a British Waterways engineer. He also volunteered to roust out the lock-keeper and set off on this dubious mission by bicycle. In the interim we could devote ourselves to freeing *Swan*, once again aground, smack in the entrance to the first lock.

The Staffordshire and Worcestershire Canal joins the Severn through a wonderful system of basins, all interconnected and criss-crossed by pathways and unexpected little bridges.

Plenty of room in the Severn chambers. The locks were built to a big barge standard in the mid-nineteenth century

Stourport's waterways. The large basin nearest the camera is now filled in, and many of the fine buildings demolished

Our schoolboy messenger was to be observed skirting the tortuous perimeter, hunched over the controls and pedalling furiously. We prayed that the lock-keeper was a good-tempered man, resigned to such interruptions.

The town of Stourport, which grew to prosperity by means of this port, now ignores the canal in its decay. To its eternal discredit, the council did nothing when the region was vandalized by the waterways authority a few years back. A few of the charming original buildings still remain, many have gone. Parts of the network have been filled in and an air of disjointedness pervades the area.

Whilst on such a low note I might also point out that Stourport was the subject of one of the greater waterway scandals, the cessation of coal traffic to the power station. Neither the coal nor the electricity authorities could offer satisfactory explanations; they nonetheless destroyed the terminal facilities and handed the traffic over to lorry transport. I hope that those who use the roads concerned appreciate the change.

Georgian basin and warehouse at Stourport,
James Brindley's canal town

As an ambassador, our boy cyclist proved beyond our expectations. He returned, shepherding the lock-keeper who, after quite justly commenting on the lateness of the hour, guided us through the system with civility. John rose from the depths of the fifth lock beside Lion Hill, to gaze at a prettily assembled selection of female legs. After complimenting their owners, we left with some hearty assurances from the lock-keeper on the clearness, smoothness and sweetness of the run to Kidderminster.

As we suspected, he was somewhat over-optimistic. We were scraping the canal bed virtually all the way, in the manner to which the narrow canals had accustomed us. Already the propeller was ensnared, by what proved to be a pair of trousers, fortunately minus their owner. We got them off virtually complete by means of the short shaft. Martin, somewhat incensed by the whole business, ran down the pathway and chucked this odious garment onto the main road.

It was at Kidderminster that we really came to grief, running solidly aground directly beneath some road widening operations. We scanned the sodium-lighted landscape for a scapegoat, but found none. Angrier, if possible, then ever before, we somehow managed to drag *Swan* over the reef. I have been told, by a canal devotee, that this obstruction is in fact a recently laid pipe. If this is true then this is a very serious situation indeed, for the pipe severely restricts navigation and, having been built into the bridge structure, will be difficult and costly to remove.

In the heart of Kidderminster is a lock, reached by a tunnel under the main road and surrounded by housing with strong evocations of Oliver Twist. Beside the lock was a pub, fully operative when I last passed, but this time in the throes of demolition. It was distinctly disconcerting to look backwards straight through the shell of the building and to see the word BAR, written in reverse on the engraved glass of the front door. It was well after closing time anyway.

We moored just beyond, or, rather, stopped in the middle and attempted to rope the boat to the bank. Martin managed to pull the bow in a little, but the stern stayed firmly in the centre of the canal (where it was aground anyway) and refused to budge.

Our surroundings the following day were happier, for the Staffs and Worcs is a delightful waterway north of Kidderminster. There are sharp and entertaining bends, many cuttings through the bright red rock, and a number of locks distributed at just the right frequency. Pakistani factory workers hurried through the long grass from the small ironworks beside the waterway. These little factories, with their attendant small communities, appear to have changed little since the industrial revolution. The view from the water, at any rate, is most atmospheric and the juxtaposition of factory and countryside is a very unusual one.

Boats used to bring coal to these works, sweeping silently and crabwise up the cut behind tramping horses. These craft used to work down the Stourbridge Canal, a long-controversial stretch which recently decayed but which, I am happy to say, has now been reopened. It was at Stourbridge that, in 1962, a rally of boats was staged in defiance of British Waterways, who forbade it. Volunteers brought in a dragline to clear the silt and the public was treated to the absurd spectacle of public servants protesting that members of the public had taken it upon themselves to improve publicly-owned property.

The sixteen locks at Stourbridge were at that time still navigable, although shortly afterwards they succumbed to the calculated neglect of their administrators. Shortly after

Above left: An experiment in electric propulsion on the S and W utilized a tram type pick-up from overhead wires and the water propulsion unit seen here. Right: The coal trade; another early experiment. Detachable 'outboard' motors abounded at one time, but were heavy and awkward to manage

Left: *Lockside stairway on the Staffordshire and Worcestershire Canal.*
Above: *Characteristic S and W iron nameplate*

that the new British Waterways Board was instituted and consented to restoration, the work to be shared between volunteers and its own staff. This took three years, almost exactly the time taken on the Lower Stratford. I imply no disrespect to the volunteers who took part, particularly to David Tomlinson who led, them, by stating that Stourbridge was a job of far less magnitude than Stratford. The British Waterways Board, while complimenting itself on having permitted and in a large part paid for a restoration that should never, in law, have been necessary, was elsewhere doing exactly the same as its predecessors. The flight of locks at Marple, Cheshire (ironically another sixteen) was allowed to decay in exactly the same manner. Outsiders who wished to use the locks and who even offered to pay for repairs themselves were forbidden to do so. The Board has defied its obligations in exactly the manner of its predecessors; wilfully to neglect a length then to point out the great expense of putting things right (coupling it with pleas of infrequent use of late) is one of the oldest gags in the canal miasma.

Hearing the characteristic popping of our motor, a lady in a lockside garden came out to tell us about the days of the coal traffic. She used to work in the checking office down at Stourport and could remember many of the names of the boats. 'Thought we were getting some trade back when I heard you', she said, a very familiar remark to us now, one we had heard several times on the Worcester and Birmingham Canal. The Gardner exhaust is indistinguishable from the Bolinder, for many long years the mainstay of narrow boat haulage. Just make that pop-popping sound and ex-boatmen come scrambling through hedges and scale 6-foot walls in order to reminisce.

Cast iron name-plates adorn the locks and bridges. The brickwork is worn and chamfered by countless towlines, steps are hollowed and the bollards cut. The Staffs and Worcs is a very nostalgic sort of waterway. Its high spot is at Bratch, where, week in week out, holidaymakers come to grief. I have done it, and I expect many others have flooded the towpath too. For it was at Bratch that James Brindley built three locks and, separated them by mere 10-foot stretches of water. Naturally enough a lockful of water cannot be accommodated in such a short section and sizeable waves regularly rush about the towpath, filling the boots of bystanders and aggravating the already highly-strung locals. The secret is to use the side ponds, additional reservoirs placed there for the dual purpose of preventing embarrassment and saving water.

Shortly after building Bratch, James Brindley cottoned on to the principle of the staircase. He made the top gate of one lock the bottom gate of the next, and so evolved a much neater system. The only remaining pitfall was to make two adjoining locks of unequal size. This was duly done (not by Brindley) on the Grand Union Canal above Leamington in the 1930s.

We pushed on through simpler but no less attractive installations and, at Aldersley Junction, took the decision to continue further northward, staying on the Staffs and Worcs and eschewing the temptation, if that is the word, of returning to London by way of Birmingham.

Left: *Filling the two-chamber flight at Botterham.* Right: *Not quite a staircase. The three chamber flight at Bratch has awkwardly short intervening pounds*

Chapter 22

Autherley to Sutton Stop

Up and down the country, hunched figures jab urgently at the earth with spades. They usually operate in the hours of darkness, for they are reticent about their work, and anyway the land they are digging is rarely theirs. I have often been such a person, in summer, at any rate, when, at thrice-weekly intervals, *Swan's* lavatory needed emptying.

We were now north of Autherley, moored by a deserted expanse of meadow, well away from habitation and its attendant harassments of inquisitive drunks, policemen on duty and furious smallholders. We had negotiated that strange narrow section of the Staffs and Worcs near Coven Heath and selected a field which, as far as darkness would allow, appeared vintage lavatorial territory. In a blaze of torchlight a hole was dug, the deed done and we could eat our supper in peace of mind.

The next morning, of course, several houses became visible while all but one of the dark lumps observed the previous evening proved to be cows. The exception was a large and fiery bull which snorted and pawed the ground in the approved manner.

John gleefully brought this information with the coffee as I slumbered inertly in the hold. After a period of thanksgiving the mooring pins were tweaked out and we stole away northward without hindrance, for the cattle had retreated to the skyline.

We had a number of narrow locks to deal with in our descent to the valley of the Upper Trent. The communal bicycle would be useful here, despite an acute and apparently incurable front hub ailment. First, however, I had to telephone London and to do so bumbled off down the highways and bye-ways of rural Staffordshire. On my return I made the grave mistake of purchasing a pint of milk and a loaf, together making a virtually uncarryable load. I can only just ride a bike down a towpath at the best of times. Cycling one-handed through long grass, along a path peppered with nettles and landslips, to say nothing of overhanging shrubbery, is little short of suicide. There were two alternatives. One was to ride fast, relying upon momentum to overcome the obstacles; the other was to walk. After a short and injurious spell of the first, I adopted the second course and settled down to a long trudge.

It is quite surprising how fast *Swan* can move when one is in pursuit of her; I found myself hoping for a serious stranding or a jammed lock gate. Eventually I caught up sufficient distance for my shrill cries to carry. At Boggs Lock, number thirty-four, the bicycle was lifted aboard and the wounds of its exhausted rider treated with the scorn that they no doubt deserved.

All was not yet over, for I inadvisedly jumped ashore at a bridge hole thinking, in my foolish error, that I would just run along to the next lock and get it ready. Round the first corner, however, lurked a dredger, studiously dumping dredge all over the towpath. This may seem quite a good idea, for carting this muck about in boats adds greatly to the expense of maintenance. Unfortunately the dredge takes several weeks to dry and is most unpalatable in the meantime.

I was forced to divert, through a hedge, across a field full of terrifying pigs, up a four foot wall, across a road, and down a 10 foot drop, into nettles. While all this was going on, *Swan* had stuck. So too had a cruiser going the other way. The Staffs and Worcs was desperately shallow and particularly so at this point. Hence, I suppose, the dredger. I stared back, at the jumble of boats, the protruding poles and boathooks, and watched my comrades struggle. Twenty minutes later we were in business again, plodding resolutely forward and wondering who had the job of choosing the stretches to dredge, out of the wide choice available.

The rural charm of the Staffs and Worcs has been sullied somewhat by the M6 motorway. A very strange and alien face it presents to the canal, although no doubt the scars of

Dredging and towpath troubles. Swan is hard aground beyond the maintenance dredger and pusher tug

roadbuilding are no worse than those inflicted when the canals first came. The racket from the roadway, however, is intense and relentless. The drivers had nothing like the time to devote to us as we had to them and I doubt very much if one in a hundred ever saw us.

In the same region we found some extremely stiff gate paddles. Martin, who is by no means diminutive in stature, was able to lift his feet from the ground while trying to swing a windlass and, even so, failed to operate the gear. In this region too, the angling societies had excelled themselves with some particularly unfriendly notices. 'Keep out or be prosecuted' is a fair sample.

Mercifully, the motorway leaves the canal after a mile or so, crossing it by a slot-like bridge of gargantuan proportions. Beyond it the canal rambles unconcernedly, as before.

At Radford it rained. John and Martin were happily ensconced below, cackling at one another's jokes in an atmosphere of civilized ease; I was steering. It rained harder and I had shut myself inside the folding doors and draped my coat over the flanges of the surrounding hatchway. It was an extraordinary feeling; face and feet were exposed to widely differing standards of comfort.

There is a doleful little corner beyond Radford, where a small salt works stands in a minor pocket of gloom and despond on what is normally a cheerful little waterway. Here it rained hardest, while the express trains rocketed by on the embankment above, flashing towards the trees which line the northern fringe of Cannock Chase.

By the time we had reached The Wide, that delightful pool through which the canal passes, the sky had cleared. The atmosphere freshened into a marvellous after-the-rain feeling which complemented The Wide beautifully. John and Martin emerged to busy themselves

A new architecture. The S and W beneath the M6 motorway near Penkridge

Above left: Circular lock weir of the type evolved by Brindley. The central grill prevents branches from jamming up the culvert. Right: *Motorists view of* Swan, *near Lichfield*

about the engine room as we crossed the Trent and made a rare old hash of rejoining the Trent and Mersey Canal. We were back on our route of the previous year.

We stopped, as before, at the waterside pub near Rugeley and, upon restarting, regrettably omitted to disconnect the bow mooring rope from what proved to be an insubstantial piece of bush. We stopped again, the next day, at Fradley, the first time ever, for me, in anything other than a downpour at that point.

Swan turned south this time, down a 'detached' portion of the Coventry Canal. The detachment was administrative rather than physical, and stemmed from money troubles during construction. Five miles of Coventry Canal alternate with five miles of the Birmingham and Fazeley, before the Coventry can be rejoined again.

The Coventry Canal is extremely shallow. I recall Leslie Morton, Chairman of the Willow Wren group, speaking of his company's plans to carry malovine sand down the Trent and Mersey, and the Coventry, to Tamworth. 'British Waterways have guaranteed us 3 feet 3 inches. I think we can find the other 3 inches for ourselves.' I can only say, in the light of our own experiences in *Swan*, that someone must have been joking!

I fell in here, years ago and now contrived to do so again, whilst foolishly walking, tightrope fashion, along *Swan's* gunwale. After an arm-flailing age I fell the wrong way, into the water, but contrived to cling to the boat as it rumbled past, and hauled myself aboard. Martin had also drenched and injured himself on the Fradley flight, by falling backwards from a lock gate and landing half on the towpath, half in the water. I have yet to see John get wet, although he inflicted a minor back injury upon himself the same morning. (After

Above: Entrance to the Griff Colliery Arm near Hawkesbury, and in use for 174 years, until 1961. The parapet has been removed by vandals. Left: Ovaltine boats Ray *and* Mimas *seen at Hawkesbury 1953*

he first read this in *Motor Boat and Yachting,* he caustically informed me that it had only proved to be a cracked vertebra.)

Notwithstanding his activities, John's general spruceness was a constant source of amazement to us. After the most gruelling of days, during which the rest of the crew declined to the standards of Dartmoor escapees, John would still have an 'Anyone for tennis?' aura. Whenever we reached a shop or a pub (amongst our few contacts with the outside world) we always let John enter first, as a matter of course.

Fazeley Junction, Tamworth and Atherstone were all reached and passed. Here the fields are occasionally interrupted by little urban outcrops. Atherstone locks were in a better condition than I remember them, although at that time one chamber used to empty almost as rapidly as it filled. Here too, boats still loaded coal, though far fewer were doing so than formerly. Beyond lay Nuneaton, which has an evil reputation amongst canal people, by virtue of its shallows (at long last dredged now, after years of nagging).

At Marston the Ashby Canal adjoins and at Hawkesbury Junction the working boats congregate. About half the Willow Wren fleet seemed to be there and our Gardner engine attracted a widespread interest. Several of the boat people paid *Swan* a visit and reminisced about their own late-lamented Bolinder engines, with some point, for the reliability of some of the later narrow boat installations was nothing for their makers to boast about.

A boatman button-holed Martin and told him how his uncle had attempted to start a Bolinder once, first warming it with a blowlamp in the approved manner. This engine had a kickstarter however, and the unfortunate uncle, upon kicking, had been greeted by a backfire, which propelled him through the open cabin doors and out into the cut.

Hawkesbury is known to the boatpeople as Sutton Stop, or often just 'Sutton', after a succession of toll-keepers from that family. The name lingers although the Suttons' tenancy ended almost a century ago. At Hawkesbury is a stop lock, a pub (The Greyhound) and a 180 degree bend which is really tight. The Coventry and North Oxford Canals run side by side until, in effect, they touch. One side continues five miles on to Coventry itself, but practically all traffic negotiates the hairpin. There are frequently boats moored just on the turn, and there is always an appreciative audience to witness any debacle.

I have counted over eighty working boats at this point, heard the air athrob with barking diesels and watched pair after pair twirl round the turn. As a small boy with a penchant for boats' names, I noted down *Cassiopia*, *Greyhound*, *Jaguar*, *Andromeda*, *Buffalo*, and *Achernar*. Many were still in the colours of Fellows, Morton and Clayton. The Ovaltine boats were there too, painted up to the nines; the *William*, later to join the Beauchamp Lodge Boys Club, was one of them. Nowadays, though, Hawkesbury is a quiet spot, with few passing craft to recall the intense, continual activity of earlier years.

Chapter 23

Back to Cowley

The long bumble down to Braunston is not generally conducive to feats of daring-do. There are only three locks in the twenty-two miles from Hawkesbury, and the athlete in oneself lies largely dormant. The route is pleasant enough, but scarcely merits a four-men-lashed-to-the-wheel style of prose.

Like Kilroy, James Brindley was here, and he left his customary mark, a rambling waterway which winds along the contour like a length of baggy-wrinkle. This would have provided unlimited entertainment for helmsmen and women, had not Charles Vignoles come along in 1829 and straightened the whole lot out. The 'Brindley Curves' were abandoned and it was along the later, more direct waterway that we pottered. Friends were to join and leave again before we finally reached Uxbridge. Some malicious beast had already scraped the words 'Welcome back Margaret' in the bottom of the frying pan.

Martin leaned from *Swan's* engine room in a Casey Jones hat, to wash his hands in the cooling water outflow. We often used to do this, reaching up to take a hot towel from the pipes above the toiling Gardner. The crews of passing pleasure boats would stare in awe as some sud-covered individual spattered himself in small heated-up portions of canal water. No one got cholera, although we eschewed the waters of Worcester, Nuneaton and Leamington Spa. Nonetheless, I'm surprised this ablutionary system is not more widely recognized. Canals are not all that noisome.

Braunston was really jumping. Working boats rattled by, hirers and mechanics rushed about the Blue Line dock. The water turned a deep mulligatawny. I met Eric de Maré, engaged in photographing pages May, October and December for a new Waterways Calendar. His book *Canals of England* (published by the Architectural Press, London) is, incidentally, one of the finest on the subject; it will prove, I believe, a memorial to the unique conjunction of leisure and utility which the Midland canals have represented.

At Stoke Bruerne we encountered the Willow Wren Company's boats *Whitby* and *Moon*, engaged on their fourth trip northward since we passed them at Brentford a fortnight before. They were aiding another pair, in trouble with a smashed cylinder head and were

The Oxford curves. Brindley's old canal stretches alongside the hedge and under the road bridge. Like several other sections made redundant by Telford's straightening of the Northern Oxford, this portion still holds water

working as a single tow with, to all intents and purposes, one motor and three butties. Martin and I helped pull two loaded boats, totalling well over sixty tons, into one of the Stoke locks. It was such a back-breaking effort that I began to wonder if we were still tied to the previous pair of gates.

We found a cow in the cut near Linford, wallowing inanely about the channel before some doleful Friesian bystanders. I saw a hefty water rat (and I swear to this) run straight under the nose of an angler's dog that looked exactly like Snoopy and which continued to stare beadily across the water, focusing on nothing in particular.

I think I must hold the record for going aground in a certain stretch at Bletchley. We almost made it this time, but suddenly, when right in the middle of the channel, the boat canted dispiritedly and ground to a wobbly stop. We tumbled about with boathooks and poles for what seemed the thousandth time in a fortnight. Independent Blondin figures tiptoed along the gunwales with candy-striped shafts and argued the pros and cons of poling the stern, as opposed to the bow. At last unstuck, we moored for the week and, nursing our various kitbags, departed for the metropolis.

Everyone returned the following weekend. Albert rejoined us as we came up on the electric train, battening his eardrums as we buffeted through the bridges. The designers of the carriages seemed to have overlooked noise, at least on the London-Bletchley locals; there must be a high incidence of shell-shock amongst the Chiltern commuters. The sun came

Above: *Iron ice-breaker near Norton Junction, Grand Union.*
Below: *The Willow Wren butties under manual tow, Stoke flight*

Above left: *During World War II, several pairs of Grand Union boats were crewed by women volunteers, here seen at Bulls Bridge depot Southall.* Right: *Dutch bystander at Marsworth*

out in a final effort to poach us on the spot, as it always seems to on this final stretch. Albert met some Dutch girls at Marsworth, sunbathing on the towpath in swimsuits and, in one case, only half a bikini. Suitably abashed at this unaccustomed spectacle he cycled into the hedge and completely failed to prepare the lock. We gave the girls a lift and reflected on changing times.

Even when you are pursued relentlessly, as we were, by eight boatloads of chocolate, the Hertfordshire countryside is most stimulating. It was a blissful weekend on which to end it all. We skirted the anglers at Cassiobury, avoided its ghost and in good time reached the final mooring back at Cowley Lock. The Gardner engine emitted some final coughs, and put in a postscript or two before the flywheel rebounded and came to a halt at last. It had run uncomplainingly and unremittingly for a total of twenty days.

Chapter 24

The Canals Today

What conclusions can be drawn from our trips? Mainly that the English waterways (like the Welsh, the Scottish and the Irish waterways) are an atrophied shadow of their nineteenth-century selves. Their standards are lower, considerably lower, than those of the day they were built. The quantities of goods carried upon. them are a pathetic fraction of the tonnage on our roads, although quite what tonnage the roads could carry if they were narrow, muddy and unsurfaced is an entertaining point to consider.

Why is this so? I am convinced that it stems from a deep rooted malice and that the post-nationalization history derives from a decision taken within the Ministry of Transport long ago. This will be emphatically denied, at least by British Waterways officials, as one regime succeeds another and the waterway system undergoes a stage-by-stage decline. Possibly the latest British Waterways authority, the British Waterways Board, is in fact sincere and honest in its statements; only time will show. The canal system of the Midlands has, however, been emasculated virtually beyond redemption and is now regarded as a leisure system only.

The Ministry, which appoints the British Waterways Board itself, prefers to keep mum-a useful and proven strategy in these days of bureaucratic power, but a shabby one in its failure to present its policies openly to the public.

Some time after my trips on the *Swan* I went for a journey along the French Canal du Loing and through to the Canal Lateral à la Loire. These are waterways no wider than the Grand Union, but deeper and with larger locks. Up and down them labour the péniches, plodding forward through the countless locks, their crews wishing they could make the same pace as on the Seine, but nonetheless contriving to manage 300 tons of cargo in each instance. On an average, in my observation, a péniche passed through a lock on the Loing every twenty minutes. Thus the equivalent of a fifteen ton lorry passes through every minute. One family, using one. relatively small diesel engine moves 300 tons of gravel, barley, grain or bulk metals twenty-five or thirty miles in a day. The fifteen ton lorry must make twenty trips to carry the same amount the same distance.

Elsewhere in France the canals are being enlarged to take craft of 1,350 tons. A European system is being constructed on this basis, with a new waterway through the Jura Mountains linking the Rhine and the Danube. A vast continental network has been planned to carry goods with economy and, in view of the bulk of the cargoes, with great speed. Such craft could cross the English Channel but it is doubtful that they would venture beyond the Pool of London.

This is the measure of the British Ministry of Transport's achievement. It opted for the railways, which have in turn been pruned viciously and which have, in any case, lost traffic to the roads. A topsy-turvy system of accountancy sees to that. Both railways and waterways record heavy losses, with interest; no road accounts are presented. A proper road accountancy should encompass the many ancillary services provided, from public lighting to the public morgue. The present highly arbitrary basis is certainly not cognisant of the social damage that road transport imposes.

All this, alas, is not recognized by the bulk of the public and certainly not by politicians who, although at this time intrigued by technological advance, seem unable to perceive the fact that every new development really employs age-old principles; they certainly seem incapable of relating economy and social comfort with scientific progress. Thus we get road haulage in the UK, an inefficient, hurtful and largely destructive system.

Anyone querying the position of the English canals as freight carriers is likely to be shown the Grand Union or the jaded Worcester and Birmingham and, with a laugh and a nudge, told how old and out-of-date they are. It is as if someone enquiring about motorways were shown the equivalent of a cart track.

I have heard British politicians (representatives of the Ministry) belittle the suggestion that we should emulate the continentals. We have been told that the European network is based on a broad system of rivers with the inference that ours is not (what then, for example, are the Kennet and the Avon?). Incidentally, the Rhine, that oft-quoted example of the superior continental endowment, features in fact a rapid current, a hard winter and in time of drought, water shortages with shallow depths.

Though many British canals were in poor shape upon nationalization, having suffered chiefly under the railways, the Grand Union was not so. It carried a heavy traffic in view of its size, chiefly in metals, coal, grain and other bulk goods. During the 1930s the Grand Union had gradually developed; money was poured in, the locks were widened, great fleets of narrow boats were built, a deepening programme was prepared.

Upon nationalization, in 1947, all this stopped. No further experiments were made with wide boats, no more expansion was contemplated; the Grand Union, like all the other

Wide boat Progress *of the type intended by the Grand Union Company as an eventual replacement for the narrow boat. It is now a houseboat near Cowley*

'narrow' canals, petrified then rotted. The British Waterways Board has claimed that this recent decline has been purely an economic one, that, to quote its own phrase, 'natural selection works'.

Natural selection worked on the Grand Union as on all other narrow canals, in a failure to seek traffic, and in a failure to modernize or even maintain. As we have seen, dredging has been sporadic and heartless for many years.

There have been silly matters like the burying of perfectly sound boats at the taxpayer's expense, in the gravel pits at Harefield. There have been ludicrous ones like the failure to countenance cargoes of silk stockings from Leicester to London on the grounds that they were too light, that no toll could be quoted (the legal obligation to publish tolls being unfulfilled) and that no wharf existed for unloading (City Road Basin, on the Regents Canal, having been handed over to British Road Services).

There have been countless instances of rebuttal of trade and of neglect, plus an almost total failure to advertise, apart from some pathetically half-hearted attempts in the 1950s.

Certainly there is little evidence of large-scale investment to parallel the electrification of the London to Birmingham railway or the M1 motorway. At the time of writing, there survives only a tiny handful of narrow boats, which can barely make ends meet.

In Birmingham, traffic has ceased abruptly. Waterways have collapsed under subsidence in the colliery areas and it is difficult to avoid the conclusion that neither the British Waterways Board nor the National Coal Board care very much. Under a complex agreement both parties were to split the cost of making good such damage. Clearly the NCB as a customer would find it cheaper under such a circumstance to put its coal on the roads; I trust that other users of the roads concerned appreciate the change. A vast fleet of short-haul craft, efficiently operating in trains behind tugs, have been driven off the Birmingham canals, with, in several cases, some extra levies at the wharves to speed them on their way.

Little that was positive was achieved in those years. The Inland Waterways Association under Robert Aickman fought hard and bitterly but was hampered by public indifference (as today). There were lighter moments, as at Stourbridge, in 1962, when David Hutchings and many other enthusiasts made navigable what was already theoretically navigable. The letters to the *Daily Telegraph* by Mr W. L. Ives, then Principal Traffic Officer for British Waterways, afforded the IWA some of its best ever publicity.

A new British Waterways authority, the British Waterways Board, was appointed in 1963, inheriting the tatty and by now almost tradeless system upon which time had done its worst. It represented, or so we liked to hope, a new deal. It was the first of the British Waterways controlling bodies to be independent of the railways, although it was by no means democratically appointed, being selected by the then Minister of Transport, Ernest Marples, and being responsible only to him. At the same time, much of the statutory protection was removed with the approval of Parliament, in the Transport Act of 1962. Any appeals against Board decisions would have to be made to the Ministry which appointed and instructed the Board. Thus a highly dangerous situation was created. Any opponent of the Board was faced not only with the wily and evasive body that I believe it to have been, but had to fight the referee as well and usually to rules of the referee's own choosing. As a result the waterways, and also democracy, have been taking something of a beating.

Things did not start too badly. As a gesture, the Board's Chairman, Sir John Hawton, who had a long record of service to the Ministry of Health, extended the long overdue system of licensing to narrow, boats, although only for limited periods and upon certain routes. The Stourbridge restoration project began and the Inland Waterways Association (now

Left: *The Grand union fleet at Bulls Bridge depot, Southall, 1944.*

Below centre: *Boatbuilding at Walkers yard Rickmansworth in the 1930s*

Left: *Painting a butty in the dock, at Bulls Bridge, 1944*

with Aickman taking a back seat) entered a phase of 'co-operation' with a body we all hoped was well-intentioned.

The enthusiasts tended to be bogged down, I believe, with the 'leisure' aspect and a new element entered in which the Board was no longer expected to pay to make good past official misdemeanours. Thus we saw the Board too 'co-operating' and making only a part-payment for restoration of the Kennet and Avon, the Stourbridge Arm and the Brecon and Abergavenny Canal. All these projects, incidentally, have proceeded at such a snail's pace and in such a small-time manner that at the rate of the first few year's accomplishment the Kennet and Avon will take a hundred years to restore. All this, incidentally, on waterways which should legally never have fallen into disuse; the law however has been amended from time to time by Parliament to keep pace with each official failure to fulfil legal obligations.

Gradually the British Waterways Board showed itself to be more and more like its predecessors. Preoccupied with reducing the deficit, it has done so largely by cutting down on the maintenance, with Heaven knows what consequences later on-probably further closures, as the cost of restoration to even minimum standards should far outstrip any savings. The Board was publicly pretending that its waterways were in good order and was even congratulated on its efficiency (by the Ministry). It gave much lip service to the prospect of expanded pleasure boating and, in as much as popular and Parliamentary opinion is at all cognizant of the waterways, has been regarded as doing a Good Job.

In detail its behaviour was more questionable. The Shrewsbury and Newport Canal, abandoned and virtually untouched for over twenty years, was savagely bulldozed and destroyed, at considerable expense, as soon as people wished to restore it. The Board claimed that 'redevelopment' had already taken place (a little scanty rubbish dumping was the only evidence of this) and it chose to disagree with the restorationists' estimates (although the Board was not expected to pay). It considered the waterway 'too far gone' and destroyed it. Despite the joky references by officials to the inefficiencies of the Stratford restoration, the Stratford Canal is there for future generations; the Newport Arm is not.

Much damage has been done by a report from the Board, shrewdly entitled *The Facts About The Waterways* and shrewdly written. It exudes an atmosphere of benevolence and concern, contains many impressive financial statistics and fudges badly on recent history. Phrases such as 'there is no commercial traffic' appear again and again with reference to specific waterways. We are not told why there is no traffic, or what efforts have been made to recover some; nor are the archaic handling conditions and the putrid physical condition of the system dwelt upon. It dismisses narrow boat carrying (75 ton miles/man hour) on the basis of comparison· with the 10 ton lorry (150 ton miles/man hour), a basis, admittedly

The severed Newport Arm at Norbury, looking across the bulldozed section and down the bed of the canal beyond

shaky, which would have restored the trains of boats in Birmingham and put barge traffic on, say, the Kennet and Avon, straight back into business. This comparison does not take into account running costs, or wear and tear of the track, all factors favourable to the waterways. Nor does it point out that the 10 ton lorry possibly receives large subsidies in relation to provision of the track and many related ancillary services. The report also, it seems, is comparing the smallest boat with by no means the smallest lorry.

The Ministry accepted all this and brooked no contradiction. Mrs Castle, then Transport Minister, issued a White Paper which was drooled over by many who should have known better. It provided for a leisure network and a subsidy, based on the Board's figures, of roughly £1 million a year. Of this, £600,000 a year was considered inescapable whatever was done with the waterways.

Some of the White Paper's provisions were enacted in the Transport Bill of 1968. Because of the guillotine, however, the Bill was improperly discussed. The proposed leisure network was never debated and the Bill became Law with the problem, of the central part of the Kennet and Avon, to take but one instance, outstanding. The public were deprived of their long-standing rights to navigation, and the Minister assumed even greater powers. It was a shabby business, with the Lord Chancellor claiming that the writ issued against British Waterways apropos of the Ashton Canal near Manchester, had been engineered to spike the Bill. Preparations for the writ began in 1965 and were submitted to the Attorney General in November 1967; the Bill was published in December 1967. The Lords passed an amendment allowing the writ to stand and the Commons re-instituted the passages denying this.

In the same speech Lord Gardiner said 'There are no public rights, this is what I am trying to point out' and '... the continuance of these old rights and obligations makes it impossible for the Board to redevelop a "remainder waterway" .... '

Nonetheless Parliament, sheeplike, and probably totally confused at a massive display of red herrings included in a monumental bill, made the whole lot law.

And there we stand. It remains to be seen what the new British Waterways Board ('new' at the time of writing) will do. It has plans for developing the 'amenity network' for pleasure traffic and for gaining revenue, although plans for maintenance are vaguer - and plans for development in the widening and deepening sense, non-existent - over the bulk of the system.

Twenty-eight years ago Mr J. F. Pownall proposed a Grand Contour Canal connecting Newcastle, Manchester, Southampton, Bristol and the Home Counties at the 310 foot level. Such a waterway would serve the dual purpose of water supply and a barge route on the modern continental scale. The Ministry of Transport has never discussed this project. Instead it has successfully avoided the question; Mrs Castle's White Paper has diverted any further attention from converting our waterways into a modern freight-carrying system which could hold enormous social benefits. Today we talk about 'waterways for pleasure' and haggle over the price of a lock gate.

A few waterways remain on which lip service is given to the notion of freight carriage. These were all large at the time of nationalization although some lopping has even here been projected. The wide canal above Rotherham and to Sheffield, for instance, was not included in the network proposed for retention.

Even on the tidal Thames, which is independent of the British Waterways Board, traffic has declined. The same can be said of those lockless waterways of East Anglia which theoretically offer the same facilities as the canals of Holland. Only a major decision in Parliament it seems, and one penalizing road haulage, will return traffic to the waterways. The 1968 Transport Act in fact laid the first steps towards doing this, though obviously with the intention only of diverting traffic back to a railway system which is now also, alas, skeletal.

Above Left: *The Cannock Extension Canal, Birmingham Canal Navigations, with the A5 main road lowered across it.*
Right: *Canal depot, Aylesbury, on the day of its demolition, 1967*

Britain's movement closer to Europe and her subsequent survival, may be severely compromised by her failure to evolve the most economical form of transport; many of us may be unaware of it and a further drift to the South East may possibly obscure it. Barges may come from the Caspian, but they are unlikely to penetrate very far into Britain.

Taking a narrower look, I would join those who plead for a Waterways Conservancy, which would take the canals out of the Ministry's hands and which could look after their best interests. This plan has been rejected-by the Ministry. It is not insignificant that both the Stratford Canal and the Lower Avon are not in the Board's hands; they would still be unnavigable otherwise.

It is essential though that any Conservancy should have a measure of independence with, say, a constitution empowering different interested bodies to elect their own members. At present on the nationalized waterways, the Minister can hire and fire the members of the Board, and deliberate himself on the future of any waterway. Somewhat farcically, he nominates the Advisory Council which assists the Board in its deliberations. The Minister is all, in fact. They are not our waterways any more; they are his.

Chapter 25

Epilogue

A final word about the Willow Wren. Leslie Morton, so long its driving force, is now dead. I knew him, not well, but I knew him, a slightly crusty elderly man with a quick wit and, perhaps excusably, a cynical attitude towards the bureaucratic whim.

He had sailed round the Horn many times under square rig, having run away from home at the age of thirteen. He gained a master's certificate, was aboard *Lusitania* when she sank and began to work on the inland waterways in the 1920s. As manager for the Grand Union Company, he commissioned the large fleet of new craft in the 1930s and had the galling experience of watching it squandered in later years.

In the early 1950s he ran the Willow Wren Company as a gesture of independence against the waterways authority and under the patronage of Captain Vivian Bulkeley-Johnson who provided the finance. Later; after Bulkeley-Johnson backed out he ran the company

Above: *Almost the end. Willow Wren boats in the reservoir at Braunston.* Right: *Leslie Morton*

himself until his death in 1968, which sadly came just before the first volume of his autobiography *The Long Wake* was published (by Routledge and Kegan Paul, London).

His boats have been derided, as hangovers from a long gone era. The main motive though was not profitability. Were it so Morton would have bought lorries long ago and made a fortune; he was shrewd enough to do this, I'm sure. His aim, instead, was to maintain the carriage of goods by water on the 'narrow' canals of the Midlands, in the hope that one day the message might sink in. It almost did. As recently as 1958, the Bowes Committee recommended the enlargement of the Grand Union and the construction of a wide waterway through the North West to Wolverhampton. Such schemes were Morton's hope: that one day the 'narrow' canals might become broad ones.

Index